PRAI

YOU NEED TO KNOW

A groundbreaking book on the Holy Spirit in the Old Testament desperately needed today. We cannot remain ignorant of the presence, power, and purpose of the Holy Spirit and expect to stand firm or flourish. Margaret has given us a gift in *The God You Need to Know*. We were never designed to navigate the complexities of life alone. Through Margaret's masterful storytelling, profound theological insights, and vulnerability in sharing her journey with the Holy Spirit, she invites us to embark on our own. There's so much more for you, and the Spirit really is The God You Need to Know.

CHRISTINE CAINE, founder, Propel Women

Once again, Margaret Feinberg gives us biblical insight along with practical guidance. *The God You Need to Know* helps us explore ways the Spirit of God is active in our lives and expands our understanding of how relational and always-with-us the Spirit is in so many wonderful ways.

DAN KIMBALL, author, *How (Not) to Read the Bible*; vice president, Western Seminary

Reading this book will help you discover the Holy Spirit and open your life to a fresh power, relationship, and connection with God. The Spirit truly is the God you need to know and the God we get to know through Margaret's writing.

ANNIE F. DOWNS, *New York Times* bestselling author, *That Sounds Fun*

Margaret is a deep and winsome guide on the journey toward a renewed experience of the Holy Spirit. This is a hard-won, joy-filled invitation to more!

KATHERINE WOLF, author, *Hope Heals, Suffer Strong,* and *Treasures in the Dark*

What a wise, beautiful, and sensitive work on the Holy Spirit. Somehow, Margaret draws a word portrait of the Holy Spirit that is both familiar and fresh. I found these pages full of biblical depth and accuracy, making the Holy Spirit shine in glory. I also loved the breath prayers. They are a lovely and practical addition to help us live what we learn in this thorough and thoughtful book.

JENNIFER ROTHSCHILD, author of 19 books and Bible studies including *Heaven: When Faith Becomes Sight*

THE GOD YOU NEED TO KNOW

THE GOD YOU NEED TO KNOW

EXPERIENCE THE HOLY SPIRIT'S
POWER AND PRESENCE TODAY

MARGARET FEINBERG

ZONDERVAN
BOOKS

ZONDERVAN BOOKS

The God You Need to Know
Copyright © 2025 by Margaret Feinberg

Published in Grand Rapids, Michigan, by Zondervan. Zondervan is a registered trademark of The Zondervan Corporation, L.L.C., a wholly owned subsidiary of HarperCollins Christian Publishing, Inc.

Requests for information should be addressed to customercare@harpercollins.com.

Zondervan titles may be purchased in bulk for educational, business, fundraising, or sales promotional use. For information, please email SpecialMarkets@Zondervan.com.

Library of Congress Cataloging-in-Publication Data
Names: Feinberg, Margaret, 1976- author.
Title: The God you need to know : experience the Holy Spirit's power and presence today / Margaret Feinberg.
Description: Grand Rapids, Michigan : Zondervan Books, [2025] | Includes bibliographical references.
Identifiers: LCCN 2024048533 (print) | LCCN 2024048534 (ebook) | ISBN 9780310362890 (trade paperback) | ISBN 9780310362906 (ebook) | ISBN 9780310362920 (audio)
Subjects: LCSH: Holy Spirit. | Christian life.
Classification: LCC BT121.3 .F45 2025 (print) | LCC BT121.3 (ebook) | DDC 231/.3—dc23 /eng/20250113
LC record available at https://lccn.loc.gov/2024048533
LC ebook record available at https://lccn.loc.gov/2024048534

Cover floral design: Susie Nelson of Willow and Sage Floral Design and Margaret Feinberg
Cover photo: Benjamin Haupt
Interior design: Kristy Edwards

Printed in the United States of America

25 26 27 28 29 LBC 5 4 3 2 1

YOU'RE INVITED

Let's discover the power and presence of
the Spirit of the Living God in Israel's history.

ONE

SEARCHING FOR THE SPIRIT

I'VE BEEN IN HOT PURSUIT of the Holy Spirit for as long as I can remember.

My parents cut their spiritual teeth during the Jesus Movement of the 1970s. I grew up hearing stories of the miraculous healings they saw and experienced during those years. They even described my arrival into this world as a miracle of sorts. They had struggled with infertility for the first eight years of their marriage, and over that time the embers of hope had dissipated. Then, over the course of a single weekend in 1973, they both separately but simultaneously encountered Jesus.

An employee at my father's surf shop in Cocoa Beach, Florida, handed him a Bible on a Friday afternoon, and he decided to stuff it in his bag for a weekend hunting expedition. Sitting alone before dawn that Saturday in an elevated camouflage turkey blind, my dad waited for the birds to respond to his calls. Yet, he says, Someone else was calling to him. He felt a pull to read the entire New Testament. When he finished, he understood Jesus's invitation as an irresistible business deal. If Jesus was giving away salvation and eternal life in exchange for belief, my dad reasoned that he had nothing to lose and everything to gain. That's how my Jewish father came to faith.

Meanwhile, back at home, my mom had been reading Hal Lindsey's bestseller, *The Late Great Planet Earth*. The book challenged her to place her trust in Jesus. As she prayed, she felt as if a giant paintbrush had painted her pure white. She experienced such overwhelming joy that she wanted to dance.

When my dad returned home that Sunday night, my parents shied away from sharing their spiritual experiences, but neither could contain their burning excitement for long. Soon, they sat together on their orange floral couch, exchanging their coming-to-faith stories, stunned at what the Spirit had done.

The next month, the Spirit awed them again when my mother discovered she was pregnant.

For as long as I can remember, my mom had a vibrant relationship with God. As a child, I woke daily to the same morning liturgy: Mom nestled into the couch, reading her well-worn Bible, the aroma of brewed coffee wafting around her. I emulated this behavior at a young age, not out of a longing for the spiritual connection she seemed to have with God, but out of desperation. You see, I was plagued by terrible nightmares—the kind you never forget, even in adulthood. These sleep terrors continued for years. Hearing the screams, my parents would race to my room, scoop me up into their arms, and rub my back, their prayers quieting my pounding heartbeat.

In time, the Spirit drew me toward a discovery: If I read the Bible before I went to bed, I would sleep soundly. I couldn't explain why this worked. I just knew it did. And when you're facing man-eating sharks and growling wolves, you'll do whatever it takes.

Reading the Bible in elementary school made Jesus real and personal. My heart melts when I think of the Spirit meeting a child in simple faith and extending such tenderness and intimacy. But then again, that's the Holy Spirit's specialty: revealing the character, compassion, and competence of God.

Somewhere along the way, the practice of reading the Bible sparked my curiosity and became far more than a way to stave off nightmares. The stories of kings and queens and prophets and pilgrims came alive, and, of course, the person of Jesus captured my heart and imagination. What did his laugh sound like? Did his eyes twinkle when he spoke to people? And did Jesus have dimples behind his curly beard? I wanted to know.

> That's the Holy Spirit's specialty: revealing the character, compassion, and competence of God.

The more I read, the more I sensed a gnawing gap between the life the book described and my little world. If the power of the Spirit opened blind eyes, animated frozen limbs, and roused corpses to life, then why wasn't the Spirit doing these things today, where I could see them? I didn't need parlor tricks; I needed to know whether these were made-up stories, like *Anne of Green Gables* and the assortment of other fiction books I read, or vibrant, true realities of the Spirit still alive and active in today's world.

When I was around ten years old, I stumbled across a copy of a charismatic publication my parents subscribed to, which pulled me in, hook, line, and sinker. The magazine recounted stories of people experiencing dramatic, medically verified healings and life transformations that strained belief. While other kids burrowed under their covers with their newest comic book or action figure, I couldn't wait for the arrival of the next issue. I began stealing away the new copies from the mailbox, devouring every article, searching for palpable signs of the Spirit's current presence and activity. I even decided that one day I would write for this publication.

My parents were nomads, discontent to live in the same place for more than a few years. My early childhood was spent in the sandy, humid back office of their surf shop in Cocoa Beach, Florida. Then they sold their store and moved to Maggie Valley, North Carolina, where my mom had nostalgic memories of visiting her grandparents in her youth. They built a home off the grid, and we raised our own food. My dad worked in construction while my mom taught school for the Eastern Band of Cherokee Indians. Midway through my seventh-grade year, they decided on a whim to relocate to Steamboat Springs, Colorado, to work as ski instructors. As hard as being uprooted was on me, I'm grateful for the exposure to a wide range of people, personalities, and perspectives that came with each move.

This transient lifestyle led us to attend many types of churches. The Spirit was present in all, but each religious tradition seemed to favor different stories and roles of the Spirit.

Among Southern Baptists in rural North Carolina, the Holy Spirit inspired God's Word and prepared people's hearts to accept the good news of Jesus. In the Methodist churches of Appalachia, with their rich Wesleyan roots, the Holy Spirit was seen as God's present activity in our midst; they said that when we sense God's leading or conviction or support or comfort, that's the Spirit's work. At an Assemblies of God church in a Rocky Mountain ski town, the pastor talked a lot about the baptism of the Spirit and had expectations of miracles and healings. In the Episcopal church in the same ski town, the Holy Spirit showed up as a descending dove or blazing fire in stained-glass windowpanes. We didn't spend as much time as I would have liked with the Presbyterians, but as far as I could tell, the Spirit seemed to work among them through groups of people known as committees.

> Each religious tradition seemed to favor different stories and roles of the Spirit.

These religious traditions, among others I experienced, spanned a broad spectrum of perspectives. In each, I caught glimpses of the Spirit at work, which only made me hunger for more. But grasping the Spirit's essence still felt like trying to clutch a cloud. And I hadn't seen any miracles. Despite what the magazine said, I wondered if the Holy Spirit was still interested in doing those kinds of activities in my life and the lives of all the regular people I knew. My search was only beginning.

By the time I approached high school graduation, my heart was set on attending a university in Washington, D.C., to study international relations and pre-law. Knowing it was foolish to apply to just one school, I filled out applications to three others and prayed: *Dear God, let me know which school you want me to attend by allowing me to be accepted into only one and to be rejected by the other three.*

The Spirit answered that prayer, but only partially in the way I had hoped. The school in D.C. sent a rejection notice, and so did my second- and third-choice schools. Then, after I'd spent months on the waiting list, my last choice finally granted me a spot.

At Wake Forest University, I fell in love with studying the Bible—thanks to a computer error that registered me for two religion courses. That's how I met Dr. Horton, the chair of the religion department. An unpretentious, jolly Episcopal priest, he had curly white orbs of hair and a gregarious nature that made him Santa's doppelganger. The first time I sauntered into Dr. Horton's office, I was taken aback by the piles of books, ungraded papers, and electronics that crowded every surface. Yet somehow he could find anything in that office—as well as anything in the Bible—instantly.

"Hey, Dr. Horton," I said, looking around, "I'm in your Intro to the New Testament, and I wanted to ask a few questions about the curriculum."

"Sure, but how are you doing?"

I offered a quick "Fine," and rattled on.

But he interrupted with, "No, no. How are you *actually* doing?"

Whether prompted by the Spirit I'll never know, but his question brimmed with sincerity and compassion, disarming me.

I paused briefly before releasing my inner zoo of fears and struggles that came from being a freshman so far from home. As a seasoned professor, he offered some sturdy encouragement.

When I circled back to the question about the course syllabus, he gave a vague answer that ended with the dismissal, "Such details should never get in the way of an education."

"Oh, and Miss Feinberg," he said as I was leaving his office, "come back anytime . . . even just to talk."

Dr. Horton became a pastor, mentor, and cherished friend to me during those intense, formative college years. I accepted his invitation to "come back" so many times that I ended up with a religion major focusing on New Testament studies. One of the highlights of the program was the freedom to investigate different subjects after completing core classes. Some students chose to study the writings of C. S. Lewis; others examined world religions; still others explored faith and pop culture. I asked my favorite professor to teach me about the Holy Spirit.

We began with the basics of the doctrine of the Trinity. I had always been a smidge confused when Sunday school teachers and preachers talked about the mystery of the Trinity: Father, Son, and Spirit. The illustrations they used to explain the "three-in-one" concept often seemed overly simplistic, as if the majesty and mystery of the Triune could ever be contained in a hard-boiled egg, a raw apple, or a three-leaf clover.

But my new studies offered the imagery of dance, which helped bring clarity. The internal relationship of the members of the Trinity is described by the Greek word *perichoresis,* a compound of *peri*, meaning "around," and *choresis*, meaning "dance." This is the root of the English word *choreograph*. This *perichoresis* describes God as constant action—one who never slumbers nor sleeps—always working for our good and his glory. Whenever God moves, all the members of the Trinity work together in a dance of mutual admiration, love, and mission.

> The Trinity works together in a dance of mutual admiration, love, and mission.

One member of the Trinity may take the lead, but the others are always in step. For example, God the Father takes the lead in creation by speaking it into existence, but the Son and Spirit are active participants. The Son takes the lead in redeeming people through the cross, but the Father and Spirit partner in redemption. The Holy Spirit takes the lead to permeate the people of God and show we belong to God through the redemption won for us on the cross, but the Father and Son are intimate parts of that ongoing presence, as we are hidden *with* Christ *in* God.

All of this was helpful to learn, but I still yearned to know whether the Holy Spirit was active and working miracles today. To understand the Spirit, the professor asserted, we needed to explore what the church had thought about the Spirit throughout Christian history. Turns out, debates had been raging about the Spirit's presence, purpose, and activity for centuries. I explored a wide range of authors and scholars, bouncing between Augustine and Aquinas, B. B. Warfield and Charles Hodge, John Wesley and Charles Finney, as well as the histories of the Quakers and Moravians and Mennonites.

Many of the arguments I read made sense and most seemed

to reference the New Testament, but the more I read, the more unsure I felt. Have you ever wanted to know something about God so badly you wore yourself out trying to get the answer? I begged to know if the Spirit was still active today and wondered if I had to resign myself to living in uncertainty forever.

Then late one night, quite suddenly, I snapped awake and sat straight up in bed. A Scripture reference echoed in my mind: *"Joel 2." What? Joel 2? What does that chapter say?* I'd never been roused from sleep by a Bible passage before or since, and at the time I didn't even know where the book of Joel was in the Old Testament.

I turned on a lamp and flipped to my Bible's table of contents. Joel's brief chapters are tucked in among the Minor Prophets. Like others who have spoken on God's behalf, Joel describes the hardship the Lord allows for those who have wandered away and paints a hope-filled invitation to return to God. Following a devastation caused by locusts, which left empty storehouses and dying livestock in their wake, the Lord promises his Spirit.

Bathed in the light of a lone bedside lamp, I drank in the words, illuminated by the brightness of a thousand lanterns in my soul:

> I will pour out my Spirit upon *all* people.
> Your sons and daughters will *prophesy.*
> Your old men will dream *dreams,*
> and your young men will see *visions.*
> In those days I will pour out *my Spirit*
> even on servants—*men* and *women* alike.

I stopped and read Joel's words again. And then again. *This* was the answer I'd been seeking all these years. The Spirit wasn't given to *one* person, in *one* particular age, to *one* particular gender, using *one* particular format. Though Joel's words are ancient, they spoke to me directly, instilling assurance and hope.

God gives of himself, demonstrating his presence and compassion, through the Spirit—poured out to all people, of all backgrounds, of all races, regardless of income or education or status or geography, *for all times*. The same Spirit has worked through *all* generations, using every means to draw people closer to God.

> My soul quaked with the joyful promise that the Spirit of the Living God was still active, still alive, still working in our world today.

The Spirit I had sought for so long had spoken. Not through ecstatic measures, but through a nighttime nudge to open my Bible and read. Within the ancient words of a prophet, I had found the Spirit—or rather, the Spirit had found me.

I closed my Bible, turned off my lamp, and curled under the blankets. I'm not sure I slept another wink that night. My soul quaked with the joyful promise that the Spirit of the Living God was still active, still alive, still working in our world today.

What seemed like the finish line of my spiritual curiosity about the Holy Spirit turned out, in fact, to be just the starting block.

For me, like many others, the notion of the Spirit traces back to the first-century celebration of the Feast of Pentecost—that stunning moment when the disciples are gathered in the upper room waiting for the Promised One whom Jesus will send. Weeks pass. Nothing happens. Yet God is working in the waiting.

Then one day, without warning, the sound of a Category 5 hurricane wind deafens all who have gathered. Before they can identify the source, the Holy Spirit spreads like wildfire, and unfamiliar languages rest on their lips. Every syllable proclaims the awesomeness of God.

Peter soon stands and recites from—wait for it—Joel 2. That's right, he quotes some of the same verses that stirred me to believe in the middle of the night. With Spirit-imbued words, Peter tells those within earshot to renovate their lives, reorient toward God, unwrap forgiveness, undergo baptism, and receive the gift who is the Holy Spirit. Thousands respond.

> Acts 2 is a culmination of centuries of the Spirit's work throughout the world.

Pentecost unfolds with a regalia of signs and wonders and unity and generosity that become markers of the early church. No wonder we still turn to the second chapter of Acts to see this work of the Spirit. Yet this is *not* the Spirit's grand debut; it's a culmination of centuries of the Spirit's work throughout the world.

The New Testament reveals much about the Holy Spirit, but when the disciples gathered in that upper room for prayer and study, they turned to the Jewish scriptures they already had in hand. They looked to the activity of the Spirit in the lives of the biblical heroes and sheroes who had gone before them to recognize what the Spirit was about to do.

Looking for miracles? You'll find more in the life of Daniel than occurred on the day of Pentecost.

Searching for spiritual gifts? You'll find them stacked sky-high in the lives of Joseph and Ezekiel.

Want to understand how the Holy Spirit works? You'll find captivating displays in the lives of Gideon, David, Bezalel, and Oholiab.

> *Ruach*, which means "Spirit," can also mean "breath" and "wind" in Hebrew.

If you're like me and you've missed spotting the Spirit in the Old Testament, there's no need to flinch with embarrassment. Part of the problem is simply a matter of language. The Old Testament was originally written in Hebrew, which uses a more petite alphabet and vocabulary than other languages, so the words often carry a wide range of meanings. The Hebrew word *ruach*, which means "Spirit," can also mean "breath" and "wind." It can even refer to angels. With almost four hundred references to *ruach* in the Old Testament, it's no surprise that the word finds a variety of expressions among different translations.

The *ruach* comes to us in many ways. And just like one of them, "the wind," if we're not paying attention, the Spirit's mention can slip by without our noticing.

Over the last few years, I've embarked on a deep exploration of the Holy Spirit *prior* to Pentecost. When we simply skip forward to the displays of the Spirit at Pentecost, we miss the faithful ways the Spirit of the Living God has been present and active with people throughout history. That's why we must explore the Holy Spirit on the road to Pentecost. This Spirit is not just the God we *want* to know; this is the God we *need* to know.

The Spirit has traveled with the people of God in seemingly ordinary ways for millennia. Since the beginning, the *ruach* has been bringing order to cosmic chaos, working to deliver people through unspeakable hardship, and commissioning them to "go." The Spirit has been forging unlikely loyalties, building communities where burdens can be shared, and delivering peace in the midst of pain.

> This Spirit is not just the God we *want* to know; this is the God we *need* to know.

Each of the following nine chapters will help crystallize for you a characteristic of the Spirit of God and spotlight how *ruach* engages us in everyday life. The personal stories I'll be sharing with you are the culmination of decades of living in search of the Spirit. To be honest, I've been hesitant to share some of them. Like you, I fear vulnerability and the sting of rejection. My relationship with God, like yours, is tender. There's a real possibility that you will respond to some of these stories with disbelief or dismiss them as coincidence.

But I have experienced the deep affection of God through the Spirit's work in my life. And vulnerability is worth the risk if it means you might encounter this lavish love too.

Now, any and every experience needs to be brought to the touchstone of Scripture, which is inspired by the Holy Spirit. This scrutiny is something I practice in life and the stories I share. The Spirit never says or does anything that contradicts the Word of God, because the Spirit is God, and the Spirit's words are always consistent with God's character. I can't explain where the wind blows. I can't tell you how all these things work or why the Spirit has shown up in my life in these ways. But I also can't deny what I have seen and experienced.

Just as *ruach* means "spirit" or "breath," we can experience the Spirit as close as our next breath, as warm as the wind on our cheeks. Adam experienced this on his first inhale: God exhaled the breath of life into cosmic dust, and Adam came alive. The disciples, too, experienced a tender nearness when they breathed in the Holy Spirit from Jesus's exhale.

Just as breath reminds us of the nearness of the Spirit, we can use the breath given to us by God to pray. Prayer plays a crucial role in tenderizing our hearts to the Spirit's presence.

You'll find a short prayer at the end of each chapter to help you integrate your fresh learnings about the Spirit into your life. I first discovered "breath prayer" in college while learning about the Trinity. The practice traces back to the Egyptian desert monks of the third and fourth centuries and is often used by the Eastern Orthodox Church.

These prayers align simple phrases with our inhalations and exhalations in order to focus our whole selves on our connection to God in the Spirit. After all, the connection we have to God is already present in Christ; what we are doing in breath prayer is abiding purposefully in that connection.

My professor encouraged me to use one of the most well-known breath prayers, the Jesus Prayer, based on Mark 10:47:

BREATHE IN:

Lord Jesus Christ, Son of God

BREATHE OUT:

Have mercy on me.

Never mistake a short prayer for a weak one. Remember, even Jesus was a fan of brief prayers. All prayers hold power, not because the words themselves are potent in some magical way, but because Father God and the Spirit in whom we pray are powerful.

Praying is much like breathing, something we do all the time in every circumstance. Just as breathing brings life and growth, the Holy Spirit, who *is* life and growth, hears us, prompts us, and intercedes for us. As we pray, the Spirit of the Living God recenters our hearts and reshapes our inner lives, answering our prayers in both common and extraordinary ways. Breath prayers can be practiced on walks or in the middle of a workday or while driving kids to their next soccer match. Though succinct, these prayers, when woven into our everyday lives, become a form of praying without ceasing.

When I embarked on my search for the Holy Spirit prior to Pentecost, I breathed in and out a prayer that I still pray today: "Spirit of the Living God, I want all of you."

I urge you to do the same, but be warned: This dangerous prayer might upend your life in all the best ways.

Now, it's time to take our first step on the road to Pentecost, starting where it all began:

"In the beginning . . ."

Breath Prayer

BREATHE IN:

Spirit of the Living God

BREATHE OUT:

I want all of you.

TWO

THE SPIRIT
WHO HOVERS

AS THE CURTAIN RISES ON the dawn of time, before the stars are hung, the Holy Spirit steps onto center stage:

"In the beginning, God . . ."

I first learned these words in the original Hebrew while in college, though I didn't take Hebrew willingly. My dear mentor, Dr. Horton, had encouraged me to sign up for his Hebrew 101 class. I tried to explain that foreign languages felt like a knotted silver chain necklace—I could never untangle them. Whether in a romantic language like Spanish or something as basic as Pig Latin, I could barely string together enough words to find a nearby bathroom. But Dr. Horton's persistence outmatched my timidity.

During my junior year, he convinced me to gather around a table with six seminary students twice a week for lectures and discussion about Hebrew. My linguistic experiment went about as well as expected. Dr. Horton had to keep reminding me to open the workbook from the back, as with all Hebrew literature. I struggled to comprehend all the strange-shaped letters and dots for vowels. Reading the language felt like trying to solve a puzzle with most of the pieces missing. I still remember my first exam. I stared at the page, unsure how to begin. My palms grew sweaty. My heart sank. After hours of studying, I still couldn't recognize a single letter or word. I didn't even know where to put my name on the test. Sensing my distress, Dr. Horton approached and asked if I needed help.

"I don't recognize *anything*," I said.

"This might help," he replied, with a twinkle in his eyes. He placed the tips of his fingers on my paper and with a flick of his wrist turned the one-page test right side up.

It was a very long semester.

As the end of the spring term approached, my progress resembled veritable *re*gress. With grandpa-like compassion, Dr. Horton developed an alternative final exam for me so I could pass the class: I simply needed to *read* the Bible's first chapter in Hebrew. Out loud.

The offer was generous and thoughtful but insufficient. I still couldn't pronounce the words or navigate the letters with their dots and dashes.

"I'll record it for you," he offered.

In the weeks leading up to the final I listened to Dr. Horton's gravelly voice read the first chapter of Genesis around the clock like office background music. Eventually I could identify words and their meanings, but I still struggled to pronounce the syllables aloud. In desperation, I resorted to memorizing the entire chapter by rote—and it worked!

To this day, whenever I read the opening words of the Hebrew Bible, my mentor's voice rumbles inside my head: *Bereshit bara elohim et hashamayim ve'et ha'aretz.*

> In the beginning God created the
> heavens and the earth.

Ah, those words. At the inception of all, God stands on the precipice of shaping glorious galaxies and solar systems and a baby-blue marble named Earth. Here is the beginning of things before the beginning of things. This cosmic story elicits awe as it opens with a majestic wide-angle shot of deep darkness, then zooms in slowly: The Creator is about to create.

In the Hebrew, the word for "create" is *bara*, meaning "to give being to something new." As the Spirit sweeps in, that which never was is called into existence:

> Now the earth was *formless and empty*, darkness
> was over the surface of the deep, and the
> Spirit of God was hovering over the waters.

The phrase "formless and empty" is translated from the Hebrew expression *tohu wa vohu*, which speaks of the dark unknown of the watery deep. Though it's tempting to think of today's oceans and seas as vacation playgrounds and places of respite, these dreamy locales are often interrupted by devastation caused by hurricanes and typhoons and tsunamis. The unpredictable nature of the aquatic deep is nothing new.

Throughout the Old Testament, large bodies of water are often viewed as synonymous with chaos: the unknown, the mysterious, the deadly. Back then, the oceans were uncharted territory, and whether one traveled by sea or by lake, handmade watercraft were no match for a sudden storm. Beneath the water's surface swirled a mixture of folklore and fear, tales of sea monsters and rumors of leviathans that swallowed ships whole.

The opening scene of Genesis displays a shadowy abyss representative of unmitigated pandemonium. When viewed up close like this, the language leaves one unnerved, if not terrified.

Inky blackness. Threatening chaos. Wild disarray. *Tohu wa vohu.*

> The Spirit waits in the wings in our *tohu wa vohu* seasons of life.

At first glance, this feels more like a horror movie than a creation story. Imagining the seascape, something within me wants to recoil, quivering and scared. Whenever I am faced with the unknown, I tend to hesitate, to practice my well-honed avoidance skills. I have an aversion to chaos in all its forms—the chaos that reigns in the wake of heartbreaking loss, shattered dreams, or disappointments too painful to whisper aloud.

Most of us have experienced a *tohu wa vohu* season in life—a sudden or slow-moving or ever-accumulating devastation from which it seems impossible to recover. The confusion and chaos that ensue can cause our knees to buckle and hit the floor or make us grab our favorite squish pillow and sob until we feel lifeless and void. We desperately need an intervention, something or someone to tame the mayhem.

The Spirit waits in the wings ready to do just that—though not in the way we might expect.

"My mom and I are going to tackle 'the shed,'" Sadie said, using air quotes. "It's going to be horrible."

I didn't know the details of the shed—neither its size, nor its contents, nor its exact location—but my friend's tone sounded ominous.

The shed's origins traced back to Betty, Sadie's grandmother. Born just before the Great Depression, Betty was raised with the mindset that the best way to combat financial calamity was to save every last item. Throwing away anything potentially useful was akin to sin; you never knew when it might come in handy.

Even after the economy recovered, Betty couldn't let go of all the repurposing possibilities that any one item might contain. Closets overflowed. The basement filled up. The garage morphed into a storage unit. Betty carefully organized, labeled, and kept track of each item, bracing herself for the unknown.

Sadie's mom, Nora, inherited this mindset from Betty. She was a *saver.* Her collection included magazines from every subscription she'd ever purchased. Glass jars and plastic take-out containers were washed and stacked for future use. Broken devices remained stored on the outside chance that someone would repair them . . . one day. Over the decades, the piles multiplied exponentially.

Neither Betty nor Nora was a hoarder per se; they were both compulsively clean and organized. But each had spare rooms where chaos reigned. Walls of bins and stacks of clutter narrowed the usable space, all built on the notion of "I might need that one day."

As with many families, dysfunction passed down through the generations like a bad inheritance. In addition to collecting *things*, Sadie's family also clung to grudges. Betty stewed in bitterness that, of her three children, only Nora helped toward the end of her life. To spite her other two daughters, Betty told Nora she'd leave everything to her in the will.

"Please don't!" Nora begged. "It will tear this family apart."

But Betty refused to listen. Like the piles of stashed items throughout her house, hurt and anger hardened her arteries, inhibiting forgiveness.

After the will was read, Nora's two sisters pulled away from her. One became so angry, she refused to answer any texts, calls, or letters. When the other sister, Nora's former best friend, died from heart disease, Nora learned the news through social media.

Nora inherited her mother's home, packed to the brim with true heirlooms, tender memories, and boxes of broken electronics. It was more than she could handle, so she installed a thousand-square-foot structure on the back of the property, filled it with her mom's items, and eased the door shut. Nora promised herself she would get to it one day, but that day never came. That's how "the shed" earned its air quotes.

Whenever Nora glimpsed the building through her back window, waves of shame and helplessness engulfed her. She knew her inability to let go had created a ticking time bomb— sooner or later someone would inherit her problem, and that person would be her daughter, Sadie.

The day arrived when Nora needed to downsize to a smaller place with access to medical care. She felt nauseous as she made the dreaded call to Sadie for help. Sadie agreed to come, aware of the chaos and minefield of generational pain she would face. No wonder her tone sounded ominous.

Upon arriving at her mom's home, Sadie concocted a home-made hazmat suit from a stained pair of painter's coveralls, some old gloves, a pair of tall rubber "snake" boots, and an industrial-grade face mask. With trepidation, she reached for the shed door.

The metal hinges clanked open. A single yellow bulb emitted dim rays of light. Even in the shadows, Sadie could tell and smell something was amiss. Cardboard boxes had disintegrated into dingy, pulpy fluff. Animals had formed nests everywhere. A family of squirrels or possums or racoons had burrowed into the baggage. Sadie took a deep breath and held it as long as she could. She prayed she wouldn't find any spiders or snakes.

Sadie started in a corner near the door that was stacked to the ceiling with kitchen appliances, scratched vinyl records, and broken furniture more than half a century old. She grabbed the worn wooden handle of her grandmother's hoe and began poking around, fearful of scurrying creatures. As she piled urine- and feces-stained cardboard shreds into trash bags, she fought her natural instincts to fight, freeze, or flee. She battled her thoughts: *My mom doesn't need to know this is here. This can just be thrown away.* But of course, it wasn't that easy.

Nora had enlisted the help of her neighbor Audrey to weigh in on each painstaking decision. The pair of pewter-haired women sat on the porch while Sadie worked inside. For difficult-to-move items, Sadie yelled a description, only to hear the refrain: "That's so-and-so's, just leave it on the shelf." Sadie wondered if they'd make any progress at all.

They did, however, manage to amass a large mountain of black trash bags, full of items Nora bravely chose to discard. Then Sadie reached an area of the shed stacked with bins, many missing lids, carefully labeled yet littered with animal remnants. Nora insisted on seeing and handling each item before deciding its fate. Sadie knew this approach came from fear and pain, but seeing the crippling effects firsthand felt heartwrenching. Nora would hold a crimson bauble, narrate its family history, and explain why it was worth keeping. With a nod, Audrey gave her approval. Perhaps the neighbor might have been more helpful in encouraging Nora to let the items go . . . if she could have seen them. Alas, Audrey was blind.

Amid the endless stacks of *National Geographic* magazines and bins of Tupperware rested emotionally fraught memories— like keepsakes of Nora's baby sister, who had died from leukemia at fourteen.

The Spirit Who Hovers

Nora wept.

In the late afternoon, Sadie uncovered a section of the shed where the subfloor had rotted away, allowing easy entry for wildlife. She used scrap plywood to plug the hole, then looked up and screamed. An enormous brown recluse spider hung from a silky thread inches from her face.

Sadie had reached her breaking point.

After eight hours of mucking through the shed, she was beyond exhausted, every nerve fried, every shred of patience tattered.

"Really, Mom, you're going to keep looking at every piece of paper, every letter, every single thing?"

"Of course, Sadie," her mom responded, sitting with Audrey amid the endless piles of chaos.

Sadie turned away so her mom wouldn't see her angry tears. She bit her lip to keep from screaming, "For the love of God!" She imagined how much better off they both would be if she just burned the whole shed to the ground.

You don't need a dilapidated, thousand-square-foot, critter-filled cabin in your backyard to feel a pang of familiarity. We all have our "sheds." They're the things we've inherited (despite our most earnest protests) that weigh us down. They are metaphors for the mayhem in our lives and relationships—the places where, if we even barely crack the door, an avalanche of turmoil tumbles out.

We try to avoid the chaos in any way possible. We keep the door bolted by rewriting the narrative: "That person didn't know what they were doing." We give it a gleaming new coat of toxic positivity paint: "Everything is fine!" We cut people out of our lives so we don't have to "go there" with them. We leverage procrastination and avoidance to protect our broken hearts. We medicate ourselves by becoming -ics: workaholics, worry-aholics, shopaholics, alcoholics, exerciseaholics—anything to numb our pain.

> When life goes awry, the ensuing turmoil can feel like devastation.

If we're gut-level honest, the shed is our *tohu wa vohu*—the place that feels formless and void, the place where we lack enough light to see the way forward. The pandemonium can overwhelm us until we're paralyzed, powerless, or permanently stuck. When life goes awry, when unspeakable pain surfaces, when the world spins out of control, the ensuing turmoil can feel like devastation.

Sometimes chaos, that *tohu wa vohu*, arrives in a wavelet; sometimes it lands with the force of a tsunami, without warning. For my dear friend Emily, the *tohu wa vohu* arrived when her father called to tell her that the literal darkness and isolation resulting from his macular degeneration had become too much to bear, and he was contemplating death by suicide. Days later, Emily was diagnosed with the same disease.

For Chris and Jenni, their *tohu wa vohu* took the form of their son Cody telling them he wanted nothing to do with God. Now he doesn't even want to come home for the holidays.

My friend Tara discovered over time that her husband had a

mysterious, debilitating illness that left him unable to hold down a job because of chronic pain and fatigue. They visited dozens of specialists, but no one could give them a consistent diagnosis, let alone a cure. *Tohu wa vohu.*

When the Spirit steps onto the stage in the opening scene of Genesis, the Spirit doesn't flicker in and out of the chaos of the world. Rather, the *ruach Elohim*—the Spirit of God—hovers over what seems untamable:

> . . . and the Spirit of God was *hovering* over the waters.

The Spirit remains steadfast, refusing to retreat. The Hebrew word for "brooding" or "hovering," *merahephet,* suggests a continuous, ongoing action, and can also mean to "flutter." I cherish the depiction of the Spirit of God fluttering, joyously and intimately engaged with the generative process of creating.

The Spirit draws close in turmoil.

The Spirit presses into disarray.

The Spirit hovers over the uncertain and unknown.

This imagery takes shape throughout the Bible. In Deuteronomy, the way God tends to his children is compared to "an eagle that stirs up its nest and *hovers* over its young."

My husband Leif and I first met in Alaska in our late twenties. For the first five years of our marriage, we lived in Sitka and then Juneau, Alaska, where I became captivated by the eagles perching and building nests throughout our neighborhoods. Unlike other birds, male and female eagles have brood patches. These tender areas of skin underneath their bellies contain extra blood vessels near the surface, so the parents can more easily transfer heat to their eggs and newborns. Eagles sit on their eggs continually to ensure they are kept at a steady temperature.

> The Spirit draws near to sustain us, strengthen us, and tend to us.

Eaglets arrive wet and exhausted into this world, unable to see or to regulate their body temperature. They're completely dependent on the ones who gave them life for their survival. The adult eagles overshadow their children with their wings, their very presence, to keep them alive. On hot days, the parents spread their wings to create shade, and on cold days, they wrap their wings around their chicks to keep them snuggly warm.

Like an eagle with its eaglet, the Spirit of the Living God draws near to sustain us, strengthen us, and tend to us. God wraps his wings around us and does for us what we're unable to do for ourselves. The prophet Isaiah affirms this when he describes how, "Like birds hovering overhead, the LORD Almighty will shield Jerusalem; he will shield it and deliver it, he will 'pass over' it and will rescue it." Jesus echoes this spiritual reality when he compares his longing to gather God's children to himself to the yearning of a hen to gather her young under her wings.

The Spirit draws near in tender, compassionate, closer-than-our-next-breath ways in the midst of *tohu wa vohu* moments—those times when it feels like the chaos is swallowing us whole, when our dreams shatter into irreparable pieces and life makes as much sense as reading Hebrew upside down and backwards.

Jesus's mother discovers this when, as a young girl betrothed to be married, she receives the news that she's about to become pregnant supernaturally. An angel announces this miracle by telling Mary, "The Holy Spirit will come on you, and the power of the Most High will *overshadow* you." This hovering or brooding represents the overshadowing presence of the Spirit of the Living God.

> The Spirit appears as one who hovers and broods.

In Greek, the word for "overshadow," *episkiazo*, is the same used to describe the cloud of God's glory that overshadows the temple. When Jesus retreats with Peter, James, and John to a nearby mountaintop, the trio see firsthand what *episkiazo* looks like as they watch the transfiguration of Christ. Much like at Jesus's baptism, they hear heaven boom: "This is my Son, whom I love. Listen to Him!"

All these stories hearken back to the opening scene of Genesis where, from the beginning, we are assured that chaos does not have the final say. Amid menacing darkness and foreboding disarray, the Spirit appears, not as a momentary, mysterious flash, but as one who hovers, who broods like a mama eagle or mother hen.

My friend Tara recently shared that during the *tohu wa vohu* of her husband's long-term health battle, she found herself depleted, distraught, and hopeless.

"The Spirit met me right where I was," she said. "I was so aware of the Spirit's presence. On several occasions, I could feel my body humming, buzzing, and vibrating with holy healing and restorative attention. I felt so cared for. I have never experienced this again, but I'll never forget it."

As the day at the shed wore on, Sadie fought hard to keep tears at bay; discouragement crumbled into hopelessness. She pulled out yet another memory-holding, nerve-testing bin, delivered the contents to her mom, and watched the painstaking decision-making continue at its glacial pace.

Ready to walk away, Sadie sensed the Spirit whisper, *Honor your mother.*

She knew it was the right thing to do, the best thing to do. But the urge to give up charged through her veins.

Again, she sensed the sacred echo: *Honor your mother.*

Sadie was running out of grit and grace, but the gentle brush of the Spirit gave her the strength to press on. As the sun raced toward the horizon, she wiped beads of salty sweat from her brow. Her eyes ached from working under the dim light of that one yellow bulb. Sadie grabbed one last box for the day and placed it at her mom's feet before collapsing into the seat beside her.

Toward the bottom of the bin, Nora found a tattered blue and orange wallet and extracted a two-dollar bill.

"Looky there!" Nora exclaimed, as if she'd won the lottery.

The wallet itself was beyond repair, and Nora managed, against all odds, to assign it to the garbage pile. But Sadie felt compelled to reach for it. She thumbed through the empty sleeves and pockets and discovered a hidden compartment that contained a folded, stained slip of paper. She opened it and read aloud a long-forgotten note from Betty, written shortly before she died:

Dear Nora,

Someday you're gonna have to make decisions about what to do with all my stuff, and I'm so sorry that's all on you.

You were the one who left your family and business to drive across the country and care for me. You're the one who was there for me.

You're the one I could trust with my precious memories and our heritage. It's going to be hard, but you're the one I've given these things to, and I trust you to make the right decisions.

I love you,
Mama

The timing felt worthy of a screenplay. At the exact moment Nora was languishing under years of pressure, the yapping guilt, and the stress from so many weighty, delayed decisions, she received a liberating, life-giving note. Those words offered a healing balm for Sadie, too, who now better understood why her mom carried this heavy burden. Sadie steeled her resolve to help carry her mother through. She also made a promise to herself that she would not repeat the pattern of hoarding stuff or holding on to grudges.

"That note is the biggest gift we could have ever received from my grandmother," Sadie told me. "For my mom, the note brought healing, and for me, it brought freedom. Through the power of the Spirit, I could be the one to break the dysfunctional patterns in my family. And here I'd been thinking, *We should just burn this whole shed to the ground.*"

> The Spirit breathes life into the weariest of souls.

Isn't that how the Spirit often comes to us? When we're ready to throw up our hands, walk away, give up hope, or burn the whole place to the ground, those are precisely the moments when the Spirit hovers over us, wings spread wide, whispering the perfect syllables to help our weary hearts stay the course.

When I look at the chaos in my life over the last few years—including wounds inflicted by a spiritual leader, an autoimmune disorder, the loss of life as I knew it—I've discovered that the Spirit of God hovers, ready to speak the words that spark light in the void, that breathe life into the weariest souls.

What if, right where you are, right now, you prayed for the Spirit's sweet presence in your *tohu wa vohu*?

What if you asked the Spirit to move in your mayhem?

What if you asked for the Spirit's companionship to face your pain, to enter your despair, to sit with your heartbreak, and to bring healing?

What if you asked the Spirit to flood you with courage, strength, and compassion for the days and months ahead?

The Spirit who hovers over creation is engaged in a cosmic, generative work that continues to this day across the uncharted edges of the universe and beyond. Chaos may be as old as time, but we have never been alone in it.

The Spirit rides the thermal currents and trade winds of life and knows how to lift you above uncertainty and fear. The *ruach* knows where to take you when you can't find a dry patch of ground. The Spirit knows how to carry you through all that terrifies, all that paralyzes, all that leaves you knock-kneed and wobbly. The Spirit of the Living God knows how to release you from the generational patterns and habits that hold you back and fill your "shed" with junk.

With the Spirit of the Living God, anything that feels formidable is far from hopeless and never final. Dare to believe it: The Spirit is ready to meet you in your mayhem.

 Breath Prayer

BREATHE IN:

Spirit of the Living God

BREATHE OUT:

Move mightily in my mayhem.

THREE

THE SPIRIT WHILE WE SLEEP

ONE OF THE MOST COMMON modern misperceptions about the Holy Spirit is that the *ruach* maintains office hours. We expect that when we pray, the Spirit is waiting to guide us. We believe that when we make our hearts attentive, the Spirit is ready to speak to us. We trust that the Spirit is working whenever we're awake. But the moment our head hits the pillow and we sign off for the night, we assume the Spirit goes on break.

Yet the Spirit we meet throughout the Scriptures is a night owl. The *ruach* not only works during the day but is also nocturnal, wildly active after the sun goes down. The Spirit we encounter in the Bible often comes to us beneath beams of moonlight and whispers to us in those unguarded moments while we're dreaming.

Consider King Solomon. He receives one of God's most

generous invitations through a dream: "Ask me what you wish, and I will give it to you." Solomon asks for wisdom; when he wakes up, he receives divine insight and so much more. Then there's the self-absorbed, power-hungry Babylonian king Nebuchadnezzar. He receives a spate of dreams that remind him he's *not* God. And let's not forget Daniel, who interprets Nebuchadnezzar's dreams and has a few of his own.

That passage in the book of Joel that stirred my heart in the middle of the night is another confirmation: When the Spirit is poured out, the aging will receive dreams and the youth will receive visions. Peter affirms this in the second chapter of Acts.

A celestial symphony of dreams adorns Christ's birth, too. Joseph experiences multiple dreams: They assure him of Mary's miraculous pregnancy, provide precise timing for the family's escape to Egypt, and detail when and where to return home. A divine dream even directs the magi's travels.

Near the end of Jesus's life, Pilate's wife receives a warning about Jesus's innocence through a dream. She sends word to her husband: "Have nothing to do with him!" Pilate listens and can't get off the judge's seat fast enough, washing his hands of the matter once and for all.

The theme recurs like the skipping of a warped vinyl record: God is at work, even as we sleep. The Bible contains a long history of people hearing from the Spirit while they were "sawing logs." Often during the daylight hours, our bodies are busy and our minds are full. Perhaps the Spirit uses our slumber to say to us things we cannot receive as readily while we are awake. It makes sense that the Spirit would work in us during the hours when the noise of life hushes.

Whatever the reason, we've inherited a rich scriptural history of divine dreaming. But we often miss it, don't we? Maybe we're unaware of this important way the Spirit works because we're simply not paying attention in our waking hours. Could it be that we don't know how to respond? Or perhaps we're just skeptical. I was highly suspicious of the idea that God speaks to us through dreams or their interpretation—until I saw my husband, Leif, encounter the Spirit while sleeping.

> The Spirit uses sleep to say to us things we cannot receive as readily while we are awake.

I can't tell you the first time it happened, but I can tell you the first time we noticed it. Here's the backstory: Leif and I were living in Juneau, Alaska, when I was assaulted by a mysterious illness that left me bent over in crippling pain for months. Some of my physical reactions were so violent, paramedics rushed me to the emergency room. Medical tests revealed nothing. The doctors scratched their heads as my sickness worsened. Was God going to heal me and restore the life I'd once known? Or was this going to become my "new normal"?

In the silence, I grew despondent.

Leif noticed the change. He recognized something was wrong—beyond what was already wrong—and tried to cheer me up. He knew that the raw wonder of creation right-sizes my worries and stills my anxious heart. So, one wintry Sunday, he carted me off to one of my beloved spots: the Mendenhall Glacier. We bundled up, gooey marshmallows (with a side of hot chocolate) in hand, and shuffled across the frozen lake leading to the glacier. We stood back from the base of the icy cobalt and aquamarine mass, in awe of its breathtaking beauty.

My fingertips grew numb beneath my mittens. Leif signaled it was time to return to the warmth of the car, but I didn't want to leave. For the first time in a long time, I felt a deep shalom, an inexplicable peace, and I didn't want to return to reality.

A few nights later, Leif sat bolt upright in the middle of the night, startling me as he held me tight.

"You're still here," he said, his voice trembling.

"Yes, of course, I'm here," I responded, shaken.

Leif had dreamt that we were walking on the lake at the edge of the glacier. The ice cracked. He watched, horrified, as I plunged into the frozen water. In desperation, he tried to pluck me out, but I was beyond his reach. He felt helpless watching me struggle before he jolted awake.

"I'm fine. I'm here," I assured him, dismissing the dream. After all, we weren't planning another glacier outing anytime soon.

A few nights later, Leif again snapped awake after the exact same dream.

I found it mildly interesting in a "he sure is concerned with that glacier" kind of way.

Then he had the same dream a third time. That's when he had my attention—or rather, the Spirit had our attention. Leif hadn't been a repetitive dreamer before, so I wondered whether this could be a sacred echo.

Holy Spirit, are you trying to get our attention? If so, what is the message? As I prayed, I recognized that the dream illustrated the mayhem I felt inside. Like splintering lake ice, the mysterious illness had caught me by surprise. I had cascaded into a dark hole that required all my energy to survive. I grasped for hope but felt only the barbs of disappointment. I was drowning in loneliness. The people who wanted to rescue and resuscitate me felt just out of reach—in part, I suddenly realized, because I was refusing their help.

Leif's series of dreams spoke to both of us and revealed the toll my isolation was taking on my mental and emotional health. We began reaching out to others, asking for prayer, and making an effort to reengage with friends instead of hiding away. I had to let go of my craving for privacy, the self-reliance that whispered, "I can handle this on my own," and admit my need for others' companionship.

Soon after gaining this new awareness, Leif and I decided to attend a Super Bowl party. While most of the guests wore sports jerseys, our hosts encouraged me to "come comfy." Naturally, I wore pajamas. I had strength only to lie on the floor in the back of the room, nodding in and out of sleep. Even so, my friends kept checking on me, offering their best homemade treats and waking me up whenever my favorite part of the Super Bowl came on: the commercials. That evening I realized, perhaps for the first time, that I had a whole community of people who were eager to embrace me—even when I had nothing to offer.

I longed for physical healing, but the Spirit was healing something much deeper—and possibly more critical—within me. It took years to learn how to mitigate the crippling symptoms of the physical illness through diet and medication, but Leif's dreams alerted me to my need for others. That awareness led me to receive the spiritual and emotional healing that comes only through vulnerably receiving love from a community.

Leif's dreams proved so striking, we wondered if the Spirit had been speaking to us this way before and we hadn't been paying attention. We started asking each other in the mornings, "Did you have any dreams last night?"

Most of the time, we didn't have anything to report. Of the dreams we did recall, most were laughable, like the ones where you're running through school in your underwear, or where you feel like you need to use the bathroom and wake up realizing it's not just a dream (and sometimes too late!). Or those dreams where you're a high-level government agent chasing someone or trying to escape the bad guys. Or the more elaborate dreams that involve dazzling magical worlds you wish would never end, the ones you miss when you wake up.

> The Spirit can use the recollection of specific dreams to lead, guide, or spark spiritual awareness.

Every so often, though, we noticed the Spirit would use the recollection of specific dreams to lead and guide us or to spark spiritual awareness. These kinds of dreams seemed to increase in frequency during seasons of transition, decision-making, or hardship. This was new—and significant.

After five years in rainy southeast Alaska, we returned to Colorado, where I couldn't be more grateful to see the sun again. Soon after, Leif received an almost-too-good-to-be-true job offer at a nonprofit in Arizona. We prayed for wisdom, direction, and clarity. Leif even spent eight weeks working with the organization on spec, just to ensure it would be a good fit. Every marker suggested this was the perfect role, and we were ready to pack our bags.

Then one night, Leif had a vivid dream of trekking through the desert. In the dream, no one in the group had water or food, and the farther they traveled into the hot, arid landscape, the more desperate their thirst grew. Trash appeared everywhere—rusty tin cans, empty plastic water bottles, even a stained, cracked toilet. The leader frequently announced, "There will be provision!"—but none came. Leif startled awake, unable to fall back asleep.

The next morning, I listened to his description of the dream over the phone and dismissed it as insignificant. Then, right on cue, Leif had the exact same dream again. And again. As with Leif's earlier recurring dream where I fell through the ice, the Spirit now had our attention.

We asked God for clarity and wisdom about whether to move to the desert. The leadership of the nonprofit had assured us they had significant financial backers. Yet the dreams left us both feeling uneasy, as if we were standing in a canoe during a lightning storm. Leif passed on the offer. On paper, turning down the job seemed foolish, maybe even irresponsible, but we had a deep peace that the Spirit was leading us on the best path.

Less than a year later, the financial backers of the organization pulled out. If Leif had taken the job, he would have been let go, alongside other staff members, right around the time I was diagnosed with cancer and desperately needed health insurance.

Most of the time, divine dreams aren't this dramatic in nature or clear with instruction. Sometimes it's hard to tell if there's a sacred message at all. But ever since Leif and I started paying attention to our dreams, we've been overwhelmed by the evidence that the Spirit delights in speaking through them.

One of the most notable dreamers in the Bible was a seventeen-year-old named Joseph, who enjoyed the lavish affection of his doting father, Jacob. As with any siblings, his brothers had a nose for parental favoritism and were repelled by its odiousness.

Whatever blinded Joseph to the severity of his situation—naiveté, self-absorption, or an underdeveloped prefrontal cortex—we'll never know, but Joseph's emotional intelligence left much to be desired. The teenager had a proclivity for being a tattletale, a know-it-all, and a boor when it came to other people's feelings. Maybe he inherited some of those traits from his dad.

When Jacob gifts Joseph a high-end designer coat with a rainbow of embellishments, he wears it with swagger, failing to notice that his brothers are still dressed in hand-me-downs. No wonder his siblings want nothing to do with him.

But the Spirit does.

One night Joseph has a dream about gathering wheat in the fields. His bundle stands up, while those of his brothers take a long bow toward his. If Joseph had possessed a smidge more spiritual maturity, he might have tucked that dream away and waited to see how life unfolded. Alas, little Joe can't help himself at breakfast the next morning. He blurts out the whole dream to his siblings, who are appropriately miffed.

We might be more forgiving of Joseph's tactlessness in handling this first dream if he didn't become a repeat offender. A sleep or two later, the same theme echoes through yet another dream: the sun and moon and eleven stars bow down directly to Joseph. Unable to read the room, Joseph describes the dream's images to his siblings with wild hand gestures and what feels to him like contagious enthusiasm, but he only fans the flames of jealousy and rage in their hearts. When his parents catch wind, even they are incredulous.

Sometimes I wonder how Joseph's life might have turned out if he'd been more considerate or more prayerful or had asked for wisdom regarding his dreams. Perhaps the story unfolds as it does to encourage us that even when we fumble the interpretation or sharing of a dream, the Spirit can still fulfill it.

Joseph's brothers soon plot his demise. They throw him into a pit, ready to walk away and leave him to die, until one of the brothers brainstorms an inventive side hustle: Selling Joseph to human traffickers will produce some coin. To hide their duplicity, they take their brother's luxury jacket and splatter it with goat's blood, then spin a tale to Jacob about wild hyenas chewing Joseph to bits.

> Joseph's brothers never suspect his Spirit-infused dreams are making the long journey toward coming true.

The brothers never suspect those Spirit-infused dreams are making the long, grueling journey toward coming true. The traders bring Joseph to Egypt and resell the lad to Potiphar, a captain in Pharaoh's guard. After unsolicited sexual advances and false accusations by Potiphar's handsy wife, Joseph does some serious time behind bars.

During Joseph's time in jail, we learn that in addition to giving him dreams, the Spirit has gifted him the ability to interpret them too. Joseph recognizes the symbolism of his fellow prisoners' dreams as pretty straightforward, and the messages as a divine gift, even when one of them delivers hard news. Word of his dream interpretation skills soon spreads. So when Pharaoh has a pair of baffling dreams himself, he hears about this prisoner who can unravel their meanings. He calls for Joseph, who promptly changes out of his orange coveralls into something more fitting for a royal audience.

Standing before the most powerful leader of the Egyptian empire, Joseph explains that Pharaoh's pair of dreams foretells the same future. In one dream, seven plump cows are devoured by seven skinny cows; in the other, seven lush heads of grain are swallowed by seven thin, dry heads of grain. Joseph elucidates the symbolic message with precision and clarity: Seven years of superabundance will be followed by seven years of famine. Pharaoh assigns Joseph to head up the Emergency Response Team, and before he knows it, the favored son of Jacob becomes Pharaoh's right-hand man.

Joseph knows that God has been working in his life, but he's not so sure about his brothers' lives. During the colossal famine, Joseph's starving siblings appear in Pharaoh's court, desperate for help. Joseph devises a clever test for his brothers and discovers they've all grown up in their own ways. Perhaps no one has matured more than himself.

The once-insensitive Joseph now weeps. The once-a-tattletale son now emerges as the family protector and savior. The same Joseph who once grew excited over his brothers' groveling now grants them pardon and provision. Not only is this the story of how the Hebrew people are rescued from famine and death, it's also the story of how Joseph is saved from himself.

The dreams that came to a seventeen-year-old boy long ago are fulfilled in ways that only God could have orchestrated. The wild saga makes me wonder if maybe, just maybe, when the Spirit speaks through a dream, it's intended not just for information or confirmation, but as an invitation to transformation.

> When the Spirit speaks through a dream, it's an invitation to transformation.

Maybe you've never considered the role the Spirit played in Joseph's life and dreams, but the Spirit was certainly there hovering over the chaos the whole time. Ironically, the first person to notice the Spirit's involvement is the most unlikely character of all. Awestruck by Joseph's dream interpretation, Pharaoh declares:

> "Can we find anyone like this man, in
> whom the Spirit of God abides?"

Though we don't know all the details, somehow the *ruach*—yes, the Spirit—has been working in Joseph's life through dreams and dream interpretation for most of his life. Scripture records only two of Joseph's dreams, but I wonder if he had many more. Joseph is a person who assumes and expects that dreams are a normal means the Spirit uses to speak. By his readiness to interpret the dreams of his fellow prisoners and Pharaoh, Joseph reveals his belief that this isn't the way the Spirit speaks only to *him*, but this is a way the Spirit speaks.

Of course, Joseph came by his divine dreams honestly; they'd been occurring in his family for generations. His great-grandfather Abraham had long known the Spirit of the Living God to work the night shift. One night when Abraham nods off to sleep, the Lord comforts him through a dream regarding his future descendants. Later, when Abraham finds himself in a pickle for not disclosing his wife's identity, God interrupts another man's sleep with a warning not to lay a finger on her.

The Spirit also works the late shift with Joseph's father, Jacob. The image of a ladder stretching to heaven awakens Jacob to God's purposes and presence and reminds all of us, even today, that no matter how much of a wild rascal we become, God can use anything, divine dreams included, to draw us back to himself.

When you hear these stories—both the biblical accounts and even Leif's and mine—you may feel uncomfortable or strange. Perhaps you've never considered that the Spirit might whisper through a dream to you or to someone you know.

Maybe it's time to start looking for a pattern, not just in Bible stories but perhaps in your own life as well. Consider that the Spirit might already have been speaking to you in the night hours. What could you be missing? And when you do dream, how can you tell whether the Spirit wants to speak to you through it?

Over many years, Leif and I have been practicing how to differentiate among what I like to call divine dreams and those that are merely reflections of selfish desires or the result of an overindulgence in dairy or spicy foods as researchers have found.

Scientists note that the kind of deep sleep that produces dreams also heals us. The relaxed state allows the brain to explore unconventional connections and organize information collected in our wakefulness. Dreams strengthen neural networks, reduce cortisol, and promote cognitive function. They are a gift that allows our brains and bodies to rest, rewire, and resolve inconsistencies.

But what triggers a dream can be tricky to identify. Was it sparked by an unspoken anxiety, an underlying fear, or the tender hope for a particular outcome? Did the dream result from the brain working overtime to make sense of a puzzling situation or circumstance? No matter what physiologically or spiritually sparked the dream, we can bring every dream to God and ask for his perspective. I like to think of dreams as conversation starters with God—each one an opportunity to bring our anxieties, hopes, and dreams before the One who holds all things together.

Whenever Leif or I have a dream, prayer is our primary go-to for insight and discernment. What does the Spirit want to reveal through the dream about our hesitancies and hopes, our anxieties and aspirations? What is the Spirit nudging us to do or leave undone? In what area are we being prompted to trust more, love deeper, or mature more intentionally?

> Dreams can be conversation starters with God.

We ask God to generously give us the wisdom he's already promised us, and before we consider any tangible response, we look for confirmation through Scripture, our beautiful faith community, and reflecting on the character of God.

> If a dream or its meaning is God-given, then it will never conflict with the Word of God or the character of God.

We also have multiple guardrails for this discernment process. First and foremost, we know that if a dream or its meaning is God-given, then it will never conflict with the Word of God or the character of God. If it passes this gold standard, then we reflect on additional questions:

		YES	NO
01	DOES THE INTERPRETATION OF THE DREAM ALIGN WITH THE NARRATIVE OF SCRIPTURE— NOT JUST A SINGLE VERSE PULLED FROM THE TEXT?	❑	❑
02	DOES THE MESSAGE ALIGN WITH THE CHARACTER OF GOD?	❑	❑
03	DOES THE MESSAGE OF THE DREAM ALIGN WITH THE WORK GOD HAS ALREADY BEEN DOING IN OUR LIVES?	❑	❑
04	IS THE DREAM A RESPONSE, OR EVEN A PARTIAL RESPONSE, TO PRAYERS WE'VE BEEN PRAYING?	❑	❑
05	DOES OUR RESPONSE TO THIS DREAM INCREASE OUR DEPENDENCE ON GOD?	❑	❑
06	DO THE MESSAGE AND OUR RESPONSE CAUSE US TO LOVE GOD OR OTHERS (AND PREFERABLY BOTH) MORE?	❑	❑
07	DOES OUR RESPONSE ALIGN WITH THE WISE AND CHRIST-CENTERED PEOPLE IN OUR LIVES?	❑	❑

If we sense that even one of our reactions to these questions is amiss, we become skeptical of the dream and its interpretation unless it's confirmed through more concrete means. And even when everything seems to align, we continue in prayer, asking the Spirit to reveal what is true, and we watch with anticipation to see what God will unfold.

Long before we can evaluate a dream, we must remember it. This is more riddling than most people realize. When we first wake up, it feels like we'll recall the dream forever, but within hours or sometimes even minutes, the dream vanishes like whispers in the wind. Most of our dreams drift beyond our recollection before the coffee beans finish grinding—unless, of course, we make sure to capture them. Leif and I had to learn the hard way to transcribe the most important dreams the Spirit gives us, writing down or recording in an audio memo each particular of what's seen and felt within the dream as soon as possible after waking.

At times, the symbolism of a dream seems straightforward. When Leif had the dream in which I fell through the ice, in my actual life I had toppled into an emotional dark hole I couldn't get out of on my own. When he had the dream of the desert, the garbage everywhere and the unmet basic needs of food, water, or even a bathroom illustrated the lack of provision that was to come.

Similarly, the imagery of a door might represent a choice or new opportunity. Following a road may represent a journey, while a vivid green scene may represent something new. A big stop sign may be telling the dreamer to—well, I bet you can guess that one.

Leif and I trust that the Spirit isn't trying to confuse us. Over time, we've learned to pay extra attention to dreams in which the details are striking and vibrant and from which we wake up unusually alert. And whenever a dream repeats itself over multiple nights, we lean in extra close.

Not every dream is pleasant, of course, and I'd be remiss if I didn't mention that sometimes I still have nightmares like I did as a child—those night terrors where someone I love dies or I can't save them, and I wake up sweaty, panicky, gasping for air. I don't believe the Spirit gives us night terrors, but just as with Nebuchadnezzar and Pilate's wife or with Leif's dream of my falling through the ice, sometimes a disturbing dream *can* get our attention. I suspect sometimes the Spirit allows them to stir us to intense prayer, to reveal spiritual battles taking place, or to call us to greater dependence on God.

My friend Maya sometimes has foreboding dreams about her children. These dreams may well be stirred by anxiety, but she tends to see them as timely divine wake-up calls and opportunities to intercede for her kids in the power of the Spirit.

Some nights, our dreams may not mean anything spiritual at all. But it's both captivating and comforting to consider the Holy Spirit's ceaseless work around the clock, even employing dreams to s-t-r-e-t-c-h our faith and awaken us to God's presence in our daily lives.

One of my favorite people on the planet, Jonathan, grew up in a religious tradition that didn't make space for the possibility of the Spirit speaking through dreams, so he was pretty convinced God didn't work like that. Then someone in Jonathan's life who *had* heard from God through dreams challenged him to consider that maybe the Spirit wanted to speak that way in his life too.

"I don't think that's even possible," Jonathan said dismissively.

"What do you have to lose?" the friend responded. "What if you try it for a few weeks? Each night when you lie down to sleep, pray and ask the Spirit to speak to you in the night."

What do I have to lose? Jonathan thought. Convinced nothing would happen, he considered the practice safe and low risk. So, every night after turning off his bedside lamp, he whispered a short prayer asking the Spirit to speak through a dream.

On the first night, nothing happened. The second and third nights were dreamless as well. But then, much to his astonishment, something fresh began to unfold. Not only was he having dreams, but for the first time in his life he could remember them. Many of the dreams seemed irrelevant at first, relating to everyday life. But he decided to place a notebook by his bed and keep a record of his dreams. Soon the dreams weren't just about him; they started centering on other people.

In one dream he stood in a field, watching a stranger chase his friend Emma. Something felt "off" about the man pursuing Emma, and Jonathan knew she needed to get away. Jonathan shouted a warning at Emma. Then he woke up.

The next morning his phone lit up with a text from Emma, whom he hadn't spoken to in months:

Thinking of you. How are things?

The timing was so weird that Jonathan called her immediately and recounted the strange dream.

"Still there?" he asked.

"Yeah," Emma said. "What you don't know—what you couldn't have known—is that I've been dating a guy, and I feel like I should break it off. He keeps pursuing me despite my hesitance. I've been praying for wisdom, and I can't believe what you just told me."

Jonathan was speechless. Could it be that God had heard Emma's prayer? And that the Spirit had spoken to him through a dream to give her the guidance she needed?

Once Jonathan's dreams started occurring, they became unstoppable. He described his night hours as spiritually exhilarating. As I listened to him talk, I could see that he was more fervent about the Spirit of the Living God than I'd seen him be in years.

One of the loveliest aspects of the Holy Spirit speaking to us through dreams is that it's all a gift. We can't make ourselves dream or force an encounter with God. We can't work harder to earn any of it. And we can't predict it.

These tender encounters with the Spirit of the Living God don't happen every night, and they don't happen in every season. I can't even explain exactly how they happen. All I know is that they do sometimes. All we can do is ask the Holy Spirit to communicate with us in the night and let our heads hit the pillow in anticipation.

Maybe you hear the stories of Joseph, Nebuchadnezzar, Pilate's wife, and all the great dreamers of the Bible, and maybe even those of Jonathan and Leif and me, and think, *Sure, God spoke to them that way, but not to me.* In which case, I'd have to challenge you: What do you have to lose?

Like Jonathan's friend did for him, I double-dog dare you to open yourself to the possibility of divine dreams. What if, for the next few weeks, you simply ask the Spirit to speak to you while you sleep? Who knows what might happen?

Maybe like Joseph's father, Jacob, you just might wake with the impression of a dream still on your mind and say, "Surely the LORD is in this place, and I did not know it."

Breath Prayer

BREATHE IN:

Spirit of the Living God

BREATHE OUT:

Help me hear from you, both day and night.

FOUR

THE ARTISAN SPIRIT

MY WRITING CAREER DIDN'T LAUNCH with a swan dive so much as with a series of belly flops.

As college graduation approached, people peppered me with questions about what I planned to do next. I had no idea. But I recalled the Christian magazine I'd stolen away to my bedroom as a kid and how I'd promised myself that one day I'd write for it. So I applied for an internship and landed a ten-week position at their sister publication.

That summer, I learned about managing editorial schedules and crafting captivating titles, as well as navigating online and print distribution. When an editor agreed to publish a single-paragraph book review I'd written, my heart danced like a kite in the sky. My childhood dream had come true. I went on to publish many more articles for that team, fueling a passion for writing and illuminating the first steps of my career path.

When the internship came to an end, I returned to my parents' home in Colorado. My first stop was the town's two-room library, where I checked out every book on publishing—all eleven of them. Most spouted dismal statistics regarding the low probability of first-time writers breaking into traditional publishing. The odds were stacked against me. But it's hard to obliterate the confidence of a twenty-two-year-old, so I promptly contacted a slew of Christian magazines and told them I wanted to write for them. A few actually said yes.

The articles assigned to me were usually under three hundred words and paid a dime per word. You can do the math. Even though I published a few articles every month, the total was never enough to cover rent, let alone build a viable career. I added side jobs: I became a house-sitter, pet-sitter, babysitter, and house cleaner. I found work as a caterer, an adventure day-camp counselor, and a kids' ski instructor. News soon spread that Margaret Feinberg was ready to do any legal job that paid cash—anything that allowed me to pursue writing.

As months turned to years, I second-guessed my decision. My friends from college received promotions at top consulting firms, landed prestigious clerkships, and climbed various corporate ladders at dizzying speeds. Meanwhile, I was a broke college graduate living in my parents' basement, scraping by as a freelance writer for pennies per word.

Questioning whether I'd ever make any sort of difference, I sought the Spirit for guidance about my future, my career, my life. I pleaded with God for wisdom and direction. Then, one morning during a church worship service, something miraculous happened. What some might call a "vision" I experienced like a movie playing in my mind.

I saw an ancient scroll made from pale tan parchment paper and wrapped around two red wooden dowels. Beside the scroll sat an ink jar with a white feather quill pen. The quill lifted, dipped into the crimson ink, and began writing at the top of the scroll. What did it write? I couldn't read the words, but that wasn't the point. I sensed the Spirit whisper in my heart: *You're my scribe, and I've called you to use words to encourage and inspire a generation.*

The image faded as quickly as it arrived, but the profound sense of calling lingered like a warm exhale on a snowy day. My rational brain intervened: *Did I just imagine that? If I spoke it aloud, what would others think or say?* The scene was so specific and tender that I wanted to hold it close to my heart, protected like a newborn child. I kept it to myself for months until I finally shared the story with my parents. They just stared at me in a "That's interesting, but aren't you still living in our basement?" kind of way.

The more I reflected on the image of the scroll, the more I realized the scene lacked the specificity I craved. There was no way to tell when its foretelling might happen, how it might happen, or what it might look like. No new or unique opportunities appeared that week, that month, or even that year. A future where I published a single book, much less emboldened thousands, seemed implausible. Yet, as I pondered and prayed, I sensed the Spirit asking me to trust. So I continued to write whenever I could, believing that somehow, somewhere, in some way, God might use my words to make a difference.

I glimpsed that image almost thirty years ago, and I've worked as a modern-day scribe ever since. Some days the creative process feels like pushing an F-150 pickup truck uphill. Other days, I'm swept up in the flow of God's presence, sensing a holy hum as I write. Back then, I never imagined writing enough books and Bible studies to fill an entire shelf, let alone a bookcase. I'm still moved to tears when I hear stories of how the Spirit has used what I've made. I treasure the chip that an AA member gave me because my writing had so impacted him, as well as the note from someone who said that because of my words they had decided not to attempt suicide. The image of the scroll and quill I saw so long ago foreshadowed what I now recognize as a divine intention for my life.

The Spirit loves to use what we make to make a difference and has been doing this for millennia.

So far along the road to Pentecost, we've seen the Spirit show up in spectacular ways. We've witnessed *ruach* hovering over the chaotic waters of creation at the dawn of time. We've watched the Spirit as a constant and guiding presence among the patriarchs, even using dreams. Now we're about to observe the Spirit during the exodus, weaving together the lives of two characters with hard-to-pronounce names and remarkable talents: Bezalel and Oholiab.

Let's set the stage. The Hebrew people have just undergone a significant transition. For over four hundred years, the Israelites lived enslaved in Egypt. A series of miracles both in the sky and on land unlocked Pharaoh's heart long enough for God's people to escape. But before they could reach the border, Pharaoh's heart banged shut, and he sent the Egyptian army to drag them back.

Trapped against the Red Sea, their leader Moses faced the chaos with courage. Toe-to-toe with the abyss, he stretched out his hand, and the Lord caused a strong *ruach*, often translated as "wind," to blow from the east. The *ruach* blew all night, dramatically splitting the sea and drying the ground so the people could cross safely.

On the other side of that watery miracle, God's people found themselves thirsty, famished, and wandering through the scorching wilderness. Out of boredom or sheer delusion, the people revised their mental history and decided life had been better under Pharaoh's whip with those crisp, watery cucumbers and sugary melons. They even waffled between returning to slavery and moving forward into an unknown future. They didn't know what would come next or if they'd even survive. Yet the presence of God kept meeting them in their mayhem.

Later, a battle erupted and persisted with another group, the Amalekites. Once again the Lord used Moses in the battle, this time by having him hold up the staff of God in his hands. But Moses, buried in office duties and people management, had allowed his gym membership to lapse. His brother Aaron and his buddy Hur rallied to his aid—one on each side—and propped up Moses's weary biceps until sunset, when at last the Hebrew army secured the home-team victory.

Through this and many other wild and woolly encounters in the wilderness, the Israelites discover the importance of the Lord's commands and covenants, the significance of worship, the beauty of communal life. All this becomes the backdrop for a significant pop-up construction project: a God-ordained portable sanctuary. The tabernacle was designed to travel alongside the Israelites, providing a moving habitation whereby the living God would be with them wherever they went, giving the people access to the One whose Spirit previously hovered overhead.

Enter Bezalel, the grandson of Moses's old arm-propping buddy Hur. While other kids competed to throw sticks and stones the farthest, Bezalel was off making art with his hands. The Bible doesn't say which parent first noticed the boy's gifting, but if they'd had a refrigerator door, it would never have been big enough to display all the child's masterpieces. I imagine his mom growing weary of having to run the vacuum multiple times a week in the wake of chalk dust, wood shavings, and metal clippings from his latest newfangled projects.

As he grows older, Bezalel, whose name means "in the shadow of God," likely studies light, shape, color, and texture, experimenting with any and every material he can find. The delight Bezalel senses in making the world more beautiful through the work of his hands isn't random. His desire and developing skills come from the Spirit of the Living God who resides within him:

> See, I have chosen Bezalel son of Uri, the son
> of Hur, of the tribe of Judah, and *I have filled
> him with the Spirit of God*, with wisdom, with
> understanding, with knowledge and with all kinds
> of skills—*to make* artistic designs for work in gold,
> silver and bronze, to cut and set stones, to work
> in wood, and to engage in all kinds of crafts.

Bezalel receives the Spirit's trademark trio of gifts essential for every endeavor: wisdom, understanding, and knowledge—plus bonus skills. Bezalel has a knack, a deftness, for metalworking, woodcarving, jewelry making, and more—the exact skills required to create much of what will be needed for the tabernacle.

These talents didn't suddenly rain down on Bezalel. The Spirit had been presenting Bezalel with opportunities to learn, grow, practice, and yes, even make mistakes as a craftsman before he ever made his first piece for the tabernacle. Bezalel likely never suspected that his years of artistic pursuits and work toward mastery are the Spirit's preparations for an endeavor whose significance will reverberate for generations. This underscores how the work of the Spirit often begins long before we grasp the outcome.

> The work of the Spirit often begins long before we grasp the outcome.

We might wish, in a moment of crisis or time of great need, that the Spirit would swoop down and give us an ability, like a magical power, to ably do something we've never done before. We may think that with a snap of the fingers or an *abracadabra!* we'll magically paint like Leonardo, sculpt like Michelangelo, or write symphonies like Mozart—but it's far more likely that the Spirit has been preparing us for years, as with Bezalel, so that we're ready when the need arises.

Now, even though Bezalel is filled with the Spirit of God and is a master of his craft, the scope of the project is too immense for one person. Companions are brought alongside to help him, much like Bezalel's grandfather aided Moses years before.

For years the Spirit has been preparing another artisan, Oholiab, with complementary skills. While Bezalel favors hard metals and stone, Oholiab excels in creating with silky, fibrous fabrics. His lifelong passion for fine clothes, fashion, and embroidery proves crucial for God's purposes. Whether Oholiab becomes "assistant regional manager" or "assistant *to* the regional manager" or receives a different title entirely, the Bible never says. We just know Oholiab becomes Bezalel's indispensable right-hand man.

> The Spirit empowers Bezalel and Oholiab to lead an entire guild of artisans.

Bezalel and Oholiab are also given "the ability to teach others." Bezalel and Oholiab's gifts and talents are accompanied by a contagious generosity. If you've ever tried to lead creatives, you know it's easier to herd cats through a waterfall. Yet the Spirit—whom Jesus later nicknames "the Helper"—empowers Bezalel and Oholiab to lead an entire guild of artisans. Rather than hoard their skills or bask in the pride of their creative talents, they welcome others to participate in the work and further develop their own giftings.

We don't know exactly how long it takes for the artisans to complete their work, but together they fashion sacred objects of the highest detail and quality, creating a place for the Holy One of Israel to abide.

The long-anticipated day finally arrives: The tabernacle is complete. After a thorough bath, Aaron slips on his newly fashioned garments—including a sash and turban—designed, woven, dyed, and stitched by Bezalel, Oholiab, and their team. With each step, he hears the tinkling of bells on the hem of his robe.

As Aaron crosses the threshold of the tabernacle's court, he marvels at the Spirit's work manifest in everything that has been made. He observes the craftsmanship of the silver and bronze workers who have fashioned every tent peg, hook, and band securing the outer fabric walls. He then feels the luxuriousness of the thick, heavy curtain embellished by skilled quilters and embroiderers. Drawing the curtain back, he stands before the holy of holies.

Before him rests the ark of the covenant, its long poles crafted by dedicated woodworkers adept in carving acacia. The golden details of the ark and table gleam in the hallowed beams of light. Gilded cherubim sculptures with outstretched wings perch atop the ark, and a magnificent lampstand adorned in delicate flowerlike cups, buds, and blossoms rests nearby. The meticulous goldsmithing has taken weeks, possibly months, of sweating over bubbling metal to create these pieces plus an entire dining set— plates and dishes, pitchers and bowls—for the offerings.

What a moment this must have been for Aaron, alone with the Lord, delighting in this initial holy glimpse of anointed beauty.

Soon, Aaron will smear sacrificial animal blood over the artisans' work. He will breathe in the sickly sweet scents from the fragrance makers and olive harvesters. He will sprinkle the room seven times with sticky blood symbolizing the forgiveness spreading to the Hebrew people and throughout the land. Millennia later, the details of this elaborate ritual and the layout of the tabernacle will be recognized as so much more—an artistic portrayal of the forgiveness available to all people everywhere through Jesus's sacrifice. Aaron and his kin lived a daily existence drenched in beauty, foreshadowing the eternal Christ.

Perhaps, in our lives, we can too.

Long before Aaron entered the holy of holies, the Spirit of the Living God had been refining the skills of the artists and artisans to proclaim this stunning message of forgiveness to the world. The Spirit had "filled" Bezalel and Oholiab with brilliance and insight "to make" and teach others "to make." The *ruach* endowed many others with special abilities for the same purpose: "to make." The Spirit had been bringing together people with diverse gifts and talents to accomplish something extraordinary and sacred. And the Spirit continues to delight in doing so today.

> The Spirit wants to use what we make to make a difference.

When it comes to "making," some of us possess a single skill while others possess a handful, but no one possesses them all. The apostle Paul reminds us that the diversity of spiritual gifts is intentional, urging us to collaborate in our holy endeavors.

Just as the Lord convened a diverse assembly in the wilderness to make an abiding place for his presence, he continues to bring together people of different backgrounds—ethnicities, nationalities, personalities, and socioeconomic statuses—to reveal his presence to the world.

As the Spirit moved among Bezalel, Oholiab, and their guilds, the Spirit of the Living God empowers us with the ability to be *makers* who display the glory of God. What those people made mattered. Through the Spirit, what we make matters too.

We must remember that the Holy Spirit works through our creations and craftsmanship. The Spirit wants to use what we make to make a difference. We may be inclined to wait until our skills are perfected before sharing them with the world, but the Spirit isn't waiting for world-class artisans; the Spirit's looking for willing hearts.

Every month, I gather with a trio of women to practice the spiritual disciplines of knowing and being known. We start with lunch, quickly diving into our hopes and heartbreaks, dreams and devastations, alongside the mundaneness of daily routines. Several years ago, Susie, who felt stuck in life, mentioned that she had started toying with the idea of making flower arrangements. The rest of us responded with a champagne pop of enthusiasm, and by the end of the lunch, we'd brainstormed on the back of a napkin a blueprint for turning her creative interest into a sustainable endeavor.

Our group soon hosted a dinner where Susie unveiled one of her floral tablescapes, which mesmerized everyone with its ethereal beauty. Turns out, Susie had been arranging flowers for years, quietly nurturing talents that had first emerged when she was a child. She'd joined 4-H, a youth development program, because she liked horses, but was soon drawn to flower arranging. As a fourth grader, she won the 4-H state competition for floral design. For decades she kept practicing and watching tutorials and developing her skills. A local florist, Evelyn, mentored Susie and generously helped her develop new skills.

Susie's floral adventure, Willow and Sage Floral Design in Salt Lake City, Utah, is far more than a hobby or home business; it's a labor of love. Besides charging less than other florists (which we've pestered her about for years now), she transforms her blossoms into mini altars of prayer. As she trims and plucks, bundles and wraps, she prays for the arrangements' recipients, their families, and their immediate needs. We've watched in awe as the Spirit has moved through Susie's deliveries. She has amassed an impressive collection of stories in which the Spirit uses the timing of her deliveries, her choice of flowers, or even the colors and fragrances of the blooms to open doors—sometimes literally—for counseling, comforting, and connecting with the recipients.

One spring, we hired Susie to teach our group the basics of floral design. Like Bezalel and Oholiab, she shared her skills with generosity. She challenged us to find hidden beauty in our surroundings, to scour our backyards for branches and ivies and even tall, unusual weeds, to add texture to our bouquets. She taught us to recognize every petal and piece of creation as an opportunity to give thanks.

> Every petal and piece of creation is an opportunity to give thanks.

Before Susie's tutelage, I thought arranging flowers was a two-step process: pull off the plastic and stuff stems in a vase. Susie ushered me into a creative world of wonders. When she saw one of my arrangements and whispered, "You have an eye for this," her words spoke life into my soul.

I wanted to keep making bouquets, but to be honest, it's an expensive hobby. Then the pandemic hit in 2020. Like many, our lives fell apart in spectacular ways, and Leif and I didn't have extra funds to splurge on flowers. I'd pick up a few stems here and there and create arrangements with whatever I could find in the wild or on public property. I even kept a pair of shears in my car's glove box and took clippings from abandoned lots and fields.

In that brutal season, Susie appeared on our doorstep one evening with a cardboard box containing a dozen tiny mocha-colored bottles that once held essential oils. She'd repurposed them as miniature vases, each holding a baby flower or teensy-weensy bouquet. Susie explained that whenever she made a bouquet, the trimmings always contained offshoots and stems of tiny flowers. Sometimes they'd break off or be too far down the stalk to be usable, but they were still beautiful.

"These are my *pieces*," Susie explained. "I want you to keep the bottles, and every month for the next year, I'm going to refresh the flowers for you."

My eyes welled with tears. Our life felt shattered in pieces. Susie sensed that the Spirit wanted us to know that God was eager to use the bits and fragments of our broken lives. Every few weeks, I'd return the vases to her for refills, experiencing a subscription of love that assured the Spirit would not waste anything in our journey.

One afternoon, I came across a song called "Pieces" by Steffany Gretzinger. The lyrics resonated deep within, making my saucer eyes teary. The chorus affirmed that God doesn't give his heart in pieces; he offers us his whole heart. I must have played that song a thousand times over the coming months. It became an anthem of healing love in a difficult time.

Gradually our lives mended in surprising, delightful, and redeeming ways that only the Spirit could have orchestrated. One memorable morning, I popped by the grocery store for milk, and my eyes lit up. Near the entrance sat a grocery cart overflowing with flowers marked down 95 percent. Some of the petals were brown. Some of the stems were snapped. But fresh flowers hid in every bundle. I grabbed an armful and raced home. I felt contentment seep into my bones as I clipped and trimmed and arranged. I hand-delivered bouquets to some of the people who had walked alongside us through the difficult season, including Susie. As a reminder of God's faithfulness, I did my best to use all the fragments—which I still do to this day.

Since then, Susie has become my flower guru. She guides me toward asymmetrical arrangements, fresh blossoms, and clippings from the wilds of Utah that make for one-of-a-kind bouquets with sweet, citrusy, and earthy aromas. I've referred clients to Susie and remain one myself. But I've also built a friendship with my local grocery florist, who lets me know when bouquets are deeply discounted so I can spread more presents of presence—fragrant reminders that the recipient is seen and known and not alone.

For me, flower arranging allows me to express what I'm feeling in ways that my writing never could. This art form has become a spiritual discipline where I discover endless spiritual parallels through the pruning and trimming, always rediscovering that the smallest pieces still have great purpose. Susie has taught me to see each arrangement as an altar of prayer, an opportunity to ask the Holy Spirit how to pray for the recipient.

To date, I've delivered hundreds of bouquets to friends and family and strangers, to doctor's offices and retirement communities, to the pool manager and lifeguards, even to the auto service station, where the guy who changed my oil looked at me rather strangely. If you're in my path, don't be surprised if you get a bouquet on occasion.

All my flower arranging and bouquet delivering traces back to Susie. The Spirit is using what she makes to make a difference in ways she never imagined, impacting people she's never met. Since the beginning, when the Father, Son, and Spirit made matter, what they make has mattered, and what we make with it matters too. The pages of Scripture are laced with people who make things that make a difference.

> Since the beginning, when the Father, Son, and Spirit made matter, what they make has mattered, and what we make with it matters too.

It's not just Bezalel, Oholiab, and their creative guild. Think of the artisans who fashioned the gold, frankincense, and myrrh that were presented to Joseph, Mary, and their new baby. These crafters' handiwork likely sustained the holy family financially during their time as refugees in Egypt. Have you considered the architect who drew the plans for the upper room where Jesus ate the Last Supper with his disciples on the night of his arrest? Or the woodworker who made the table they gathered around? Or the harvesters who processed the oil that provided light on that gloomy night? Or the potter who fashioned the plates and chalices? The vintner who picked and plucked and smashed and strained and blended the grapes for the wine? The baker who kneaded the dough for the loaf Jesus held in his hands and tore in two as he instructed his disciples, "Do this in remembrance of me"?

Have you considered those who sewed the curtain in the temple and would have been astonished to learn that at Jesus's death it tore in two? Or the masons who shaped a heavy round stone for the sealing of a tomb and would have been flabbergasted to learn that at Jesus's resurrection the rock inexplicably rolled back?

Flowers and words might not spark the same joy in your life as they do in mine, but there are so many other items you can make. Perhaps you can knit soft scarves that warm necks, or craft quilts that make kids feel safe and snuggly. Maybe you pour candles that brighten the darkest of nights or sew adorable felt animals that deliver joy. Or perhaps your talent lies in baking casseroles that fill more than just bellies—they nourish souls with hope.

> What we think is "just" a hobby, the Spirit can make holy.

I have a friend who makes everything more organized, and through his work, the Spirit breathes peace into my life. Another friend makes powerful spreadsheets, and her work steadies my soul. One dear friend specializes in making calligraphy. When she writes my name, it makes me feel seen and known, like I matter. My friend Mindy makes makeup bags and purses, and whenever I carry them, I feel cherished. I have a long-time friend, Carol, who has a knack for making connections between strangers, and through them, the Spirit builds life-giving community and meets critical needs.

Whatever you dream of creating can change someone's life. Even when (or perhaps especially when) what you make is lumpy, bumpy, or imperfect, the Spirit can use it mightily.

What you make matters. The next time you find yourself questioning whether this is true, just remember Bezalel and Oholiab. If the Spirit can use artisans to set the stage for atonement, the forgiveness of sins, and worship in the middle of the desert, then what might the Holy Spirit want to make through you right here, right now, with what you have?

What we think is "just" a hobby, the Spirit can make holy. What we think is insignificant, the Spirit can use to make a lasting impact. What we think doesn't matter, the Spirit can use to make a life-changing difference.

Since the Trinity's first dance at creation, God has been delighting in all that's made. God knows matter matters. And God loves using what we make to reveal the depths of his lavish love to the world.

 Breath Prayer

BREATHE IN:

Spirit of the Living God

BREATHE OUT:

Use what I make to make a difference.

FIVE

THE SPIRIT WHO WEARS US WELL

ONE OF THE MOST CAPTIVATING facets of the Spirit is how the *ruach* works behind the scenes drawing people's hearts back to God. Consider the story of Jonah, a reluctant preacher who arrives in Nineveh doused in *eau de fishguts* with an attitude that matches his scent. He delivers one of the briefest, most begrudging sermons of all time: "Forty more days and Nineveh will be overthrown!" It's all doom and gloom, without hope or redemption. Yet something mysterious happens through those eight words, triggering over one hundred thousand Ninevites to turn to God in a salvific tsunami.

Or consider the leadership of Hezekiah, who refuses to become like his father, one of Israel's stinky rotten kings. Hezekiah gives the temple a long-overdue deep cleaning before hosting an epic idol-smashing party. *Opa!* Thanks to Hezekiah's efforts, spiritual renewal sweeps through Judah, reinvigorating passion for the Torah and leading to the first national celebration of Passover since Solomon's reign.

Then there's Nehemiah, who leads the people to rebuild Jerusalem's city walls in a record-breaking fifty-two days, restoring to Israel the holy city they can call home. Or the prophet Ezra, who reads from dusty Torah scrolls and witnesses people's hard hearts crack open like ripe coconuts, leading to a wave of celebration, mourning, repentance, and revival.

Though the Spirit is never explicitly identified in these biblical spiritual renewals, the scenes burst with the Spirit's handiwork—people returning to God in beautiful and profound expressions. Now there's a pattern of the Spirit manifesting in punctuated ways in particular times and places throughout history.

One of my favorite examples involves an eighteenth-century twentysomething, Count Zinzendorf, who opened his home as a safehouse for refugees from across Europe. He permitted them to build a village on the corner of his property, and the growing community, who later become known as Moravians, launched an around-the-clock prayer movement that lasted over one hundred years.

The First Great Awakening began with Jonathan Edwards, a young church leader frustrated by the apathy toward God's Word he encountered while preaching at his grandfather's church. Then in 1733, following a Spirit-inspired sermon, hundreds in the congregation came to faith. The revival spread like wildfire across New England, with more than fifty thousand people being added to churches in the region, whose total population was around three hundred thousand.

Half a century later, the Second Great Awakening emerged with decentralized leadership and geography. It spread from New England through the Midwest via traveling preachers gathering audiences under tents with sawdust-covered floors.

In 1904, Annie Florence Evans stood up at a pastors' conference in New Quay, Wales, and declared, "I love Jesus with all my heart." The Spirit rested on her tongue that day, and her simple words floored everyone within earshot. Those seven words ignited the Welsh Revival, leading to more than one hundred thousand people following Jesus in under twelve months.

> "I love Jesus with all my heart"—those seven words ignited the Welsh Revival.

Two years later, William Joseph Seymour's house church in Los Angeles experienced the Holy Spirit so profoundly that a large crowd gathered, and the front porch collapsed under the weight. Fortunately, no one was injured. The church needed a new location and found an abandoned building at 312 Azusa Street. What became known as the Azusa Street Revival shattered racial divides and empowered women, previously sidelined in male-dominated churches, to use their gifts, laying the foundation for Pentecostalism's global spread in the twenty-first century.

More recently, the Jesus Movement sparked a renewal of faith for believers around the world in the late 1960s. Countless Christians, many in tie-dyed tops and bell-bottom jeans, came to faith through this movement—including my own parents.

I've long been fascinated by those times in history when the Spirit seems more easily recognized. While living in Steamboat Springs, Colorado, writing dime-a-word articles, I started hearing rumors of a revival happening at a church in Florida's panhandle. Some of my parents' friends had even visited the church and shared stories of crowds lining up for admittance as early as 4 a.m. for the 7 p.m. service. They described people with incurable illnesses being healed—the very miracles of the Spirit I'd longed to see since I was a girl.

"What we saw changed us," they said. "We're going to move there."

My parents and I stared in disbelief, thinking, *You're going to uproot your lives and move from Colorado to Florida with children in tow? Because of a revival?* Whatever they had encountered must have been miraculous.

"Once we're settled, you can visit anytime," they said.

Three months later, I boarded a plane bound for Pensacola, Florida. Upon landing, I drove straight to the address I'd written down. What I witnessed there stunned me. Church buses from around the nation filled the parking lot. Spontaneous worship broke out among those standing in the long, coiling line. Strangers shared food and water with each other, trading stories about the ways the Spirit had moved in their lives. It felt like spiritual tailgating.

When the doors opened, I scrambled for a seat. People packed into the pews like tinned fish. Behind the oversized pulpit sat a curtained baptismal tank with a metal cross hanging above. Several rows of choir chairs had been converted into overflow seating for the crowd. The atmosphere was pregnant with expectation.

Worship preceded a fiery, saliva-spitting sermon that ended with the preacher pleading with everyone to "get right with God," prompting throngs of people to rush down the aisles to the foot of the pulpit. The carpet disappeared under a blanket of bodies, some bowed down or laid flat, some weeping, some shaking, some crying out to God. Trained church members prayed with those who'd come forward. In the middle of the whirlwind, I stood speechless, having never seen anything like this. I felt drawn to be a part of it.

Three years had transpired since I'd moved into my parents' basement post-college, and I figured it was time for a fresh start somewhere new. I flew back to Colorado, stuffed everything I owned into my rusty red Subaru station wagon, drove across the country, and enrolled in the brand-new Brownsville Revival School of Ministry that the Pensacola church had started.

I'll never forget that year. I witnessed first-hand God's transforming power. I met a wheelchair-bound woman who now skipped down the sidewalk. One of the fellow students I befriended had been a drug lord until his radical encounter with Jesus at the revival. Now he was training to be a pastor. These stories and experiences breathed fresh  life and faith into me. The Spirit was still hovering over our world, moving in our mayhem and working miracles that boggled my mind. I prayed expectantly again, gathering regularly with other believers to confess our struggles and pray for each other.

> The Spirit worked miracles that boggled my mind.

Yet amidst the spiritual revival, I began to feel an unsettling dissonance that I couldn't ignore. Even as new life sprouted within me, something inside me also began to die.

Soon after I arrived, a fellow student, identifiable by his collared shirt with the ministry school's name stitched on the chest, introduced himself to me by announcing, "Your shorts are too short!"

I stared at the stranger, skinny as an Arizona cactus with a prickly personality to match. "What are you talking about?" I asked.

"Your shorts are just above your knees, and they need to be below the knees if you're going to remain a student here," he said imperiously.

"Okey dokey," I said.

Turns out he wasn't the only student who, without any authority, seemed to take pleasure in enforcing the rules. From all accounts, the school started by erring on the side of freedom, but some students abused the privileges, so new rules were created. The cycle continued until rules were written for everything from clothes and hair to housing and curfew. Meanwhile, the church added its own rules, compounding the legalistic atmosphere:

Rules

1. No dating your first semester.

2. No entering the threshold of the opposite gender's residence without a married couple present.

3. No sleeveless shirts.

4. No jeans at church or school.

5. No excessive makeup.

6. No watching R-rated movies.

7. Oh so many more!

I heard stories of people being expelled for eating lunch in the home of someone of the opposite gender. A student might be in your class every day for three months and then—*poof!*—gone with no explanation. And the real kicker was that the rules lacked age limits. Imagine you're a sixty-five-year-old widow needing help moving a couch on a 105-degree, hot-and-humid-as-the-devil's-armpit day, but all the able-bodied males are prohibited from entering your living space to help.

The school even tried to regulate where students could live in the greater Pensacola area, designating certain neighborhoods for men and others for women. My friend Isabel, with her spring-loaded personality charged with voltage, raised an important discrepancy with the school's pastoral care staff.

"The places where the girls have to live are three hundred dollars more per month compared to where the guys live," Isabel explained.

"Maybe God is using this to teach the women how to pray for their finances," the pastoral staff member replied.

Spunky Isabel left feeling deflated.

A pattern emerged of professors trotting students out onstage for public acknowledgment of those who had performed the greatest spiritual feats of fasting, service, or perfect attendance. These students' stories became our baseline, and anything "less" triggered rippling waves of guilt. I even remember a professor telling us that if we weren't praying at least an hour a day, we couldn't expect God to *really* do anything through us. Since he prayed "hours" a day, we should too.

I still worked full-time as a freelance writer, so I had an overloaded schedule. Though I only enrolled in a single class, the school required church attendance on Sunday mornings and four nights a week, with most services running anywhere from three to five hours. During "free nights," the school hosted special services with renowned scholars, Bible teachers, and evangelists presented as "once-in-a-lifetime" events. Attendance was optional, but the community noted who showed up and who skipped.

My friends and I attended church services six to seven nights a week. I was learning and growing, but I was also becoming spiritually fatigued—not just from the schedule, but from the compounding rules, demands, and expectations. Balancing full-time work with my one class proved challenging, especially with over twenty hours per week of required church and chapel attendance. Struggling with burnout, I visited the school's pastoral care office to discuss my situation and see if I could get a reprieve.

"Rules are rules," the advisor told me. "Attendance is required—no exceptions."

That's when I discovered the shadow side of what can happen in faith communities. The Spirit is undeniably at work, but when ambitious people with ruthless work ethics create systems bent toward productivity, efficiency, and control, then the antidote to any ailment becomes *study the Bible more, pray more, evangelize more, volunteer more, give more, do more, be more, and accomplish more in God's kingdom.* Over time, it feels less like a work *of* the Spirit and more like work *for* the Spirit.

The Spirit was being turned into a commodity at the school. I noticed that the evening revival services were engineered with almost the exact same elements every night to try to recreate what had happened on the first night of the revival: The same preacher. The same fiery tone. The same woman singing the same song. Through this quiet commodification, the outpouring of God's Spirit became something to work for, to win by effort, to engineer through particular protocols.

During the year I spent in Pensacola, I continued to pursue the Spirit yet felt weighed down by all the school's extrabiblical ordinances and cumbersome codes. I followed most of the rules, including buying a new pair of longer Bermuda shorts, but ended that year of "revival" exhausted and empty inside. Then, to make matters worse, some of the leaders' cravings for power and control led to the ministry school splitting in two, leaving hurt and brokenness among students and staff. When I packed up my Subaru and headed back to Colorado at the end of the year, I didn't know if I'd ever step foot into a church again.

After the Israelites spend decades adrift in an ocean of sand, their arrival in the promised land doesn't live up to their expectations either. Instead of a spiritual fiesta and siesta, they awake to a long slog against foreign armies. This time in Israel's history is known as the Judges, and by the time we meet a man named Gideon, the heartless, brutal Midianites have forced God's people into grinding poverty.

Whenever the Israelites, including Gideon's family, attempt to grow food, the Midianites and their allies, the Amalekites, descend like swarms of locusts, wrecking the land and obliterating the crops. They slaughter every animal they can find, cutting off the Israelites' food sources and their means of worship through grain and meat offerings.

With Cruella de Vil–like coldheartedness, the Midianites travel with extra food and cattle in tow. They throw grand celebratory feasts, refusing to share any scraps with the emaciated Israelites. This cycle repeats itself for seven long years, until the Israelites' cry of desperation becomes a chorus. So God sends a nameless prophet to remind them of the Lord's power and faithfulness, as well as their failure to obey:

> This is what the LORD, the God of Israel, says: I
> *brought* you up out of Egypt, out of the land of
> slavery. I *rescued* you from the hand of the Egyptians.

And I *delivered* you from the hand of all your
oppressors; I *drove* them out before you and *gave* you
their land. I *said* to you, "I am the LORD your God;
do not worship the gods of the Amorites, in whose
land you live." But you have not listened to me.

This prophecy's strong verbs signal God's active engagement
in his people's lives. Miracles are the radical kindness of God
on display, and the Lord has been *bringing, rescuing, delivering,
driving, giving,* and *speaking.*

Yet the Israelites have developed a bad case
of spiritual amnesia. Their hearts have grown
callous as they've been seduced by the critter
gods of the Amorites.

> Miracles are
> the radical
> kindness of
> God on display.

It's easy to wag fingers and click tongues at *those* Israelites. But
counterfeit gods have a way of slipping into our lives too. When
we're vulnerable or desperate or simply not paying attention,
idols lure us with empty promises that if we accomplish more
or behave a particular way, we'll attain what we want most
in life. Soon, off we go to meet their exhausting demands,
unaware that they're distracting us from lavishly loving others
as God lavishly loved us. By the time we realize our idols are
fake and phony, we're so far off the path that we struggle to
find our way back.

As with us, the Israelites have wandered completely off-map.
That's when God sends an angel to an unlikely candidate,
Gideon. This young man works alongside his family to gather
and stash food to survive. One afternoon, after gleaning whatever wheat hasn't been reduced to ash, he finds the perfect
hiding place to process the grain: a hole in the ground in the

form of a winepress. It's easy to envision Gideon alone in the trench, treading the wheat bundles to gather the precious food for his family, occasionally peeking out to ensure he hasn't been spied by the enemy.

Then an angel of God appears with a greeting: "The LORD is with you, mighty warrior." Gideon appears unfazed by the messenger, not even a blink, but he furrows his brow at the notion that God is with him. He questions why all the current hardships have befallen the Israelites: *Excuse me, but if God is really with me, then why has all this happened? If God is with all of us, then why isn't he performing mighty miracles like he did in Egypt? If you look at all these Midianites, Mr. Angel, it's clear that God is playing for the other team. He is not with us; he's long gone.*

Without addressing a single one of Gideon's concerns, the angel instructs him, "Go in the strength you have and save Israel out of Midian's hand. Am I not sending you?"

Much like Moses, Gideon is flush with self-doubt and balks at his commissioning. The whole premise seems ridiculous: God wants to use the runt of a family from Israel's tiniest tribe to overcome the big bad Midianites? To prove the Almighty is behind this far-fetched instruction, Gideon requests a sign, and then he prepares a meal so the angel can think on it. Gideon butchers one of the few young goats his family has managed to keep hidden. He then takes a liberal amount of flour—over half a bushel—to knead into dough and bake into bread.

It's all quite peculiar, offering an angel a sacred feast in a time of severe famine. But it gets even stranger. The angel instructs Gideon to dump the meat and bread on a rock and pour the savory broth atop. The wastefulness is unthinkable, but Gideon doesn't flinch. The angel extends a long stick toward the meal; blazing fire erupts from the rock, consuming the food. Just like that, the angel vanishes, leaving Gideon standing before the charred remnants, grappling with the daunting reality of having seen an angel of the Lord face-to-face.

Gideon receives reassurance that he won't die and responds by building an altar called "The Lord Is Peace." The same night, the Lord instructs Gideon to tear down his father's altars to Baal and the nearby Asherah pole. God then tells him to build a proper altar using the wood from the pole as kindling, and to sacrifice a bull from his father's treasured herd. Knowing this will ignite the fury of his family and fellow Israelites, Gideon waits until nightfall to complete his assignment. The next morning, enraged townspeople are ready to tear Gideon to shreds.

But Gideon's father, Joash, rises to the occasion and defends his vulnerable son against the crowds. Barely able to catch his breath after this wild turn of events, Gideon soon reels from an alarming news report: The Midianites, Amalekites, and all their allies are ready to attack. Just as panic sweeps in, so does the Holy Spirit:

> *Then the Spirit of the Lord came on Gideon,* and he
> blew a trumpet, summoning the Abiezrites to follow
> him. He sent messengers throughout Manasseh,
> calling them to arms, and also into Asher, Zebulun
> and Naphtali, so that they too went up to meet them.

Many translations record that the Holy Spirit came on Gideon, but in the Hebrew, the phrase literally means that the Spirit of the Lord "clothed himself with Gideon." The Spirit's presence and power rest in and on Gideon as the *ruach* both empowers and surrounds him. The Hebrew text depicts this as being like clothing. The passage can be interpreted as the Spirit clothing Gideon, but some have understood this verse to mean that the Spirit wore Gideon like a garment. What captivating imagery!

Notice that the Spirit doesn't suddenly transform Gideon into something he's not. Gideon doesn't become a superhero or overnight military guru. He doesn't complete 147 tasks, wear longer shorts, or pray for an hour every day. Instead, *God's Spirit does the work* to save Israel. Gideon is merely the means through which the Spirit does it. The same Spirit who broods during creation, who delights in everything that's made, who knows Gideon more intimately than he knows himself, covers him, inhabits him, and wears him like a garment.

> The Spirit wears Gideon like a garment.

"If *you* will save Israel by my hand as *you* have promised," Gideon says to the Spirit.

Gideon knows that someone else, namely God, is the one driving everything, and he's just along for the ride. Still, he needs more assurance as he trembles at the thought of ravenous enemies. He asks God to dampen a wool fleece with fresh dew while leaving everything else around it dry. God performs the sign just as Gideon requests.

It's a convincing feat, but Gideon is the type to run back into the house nineteen times to make sure the oven is off. Naturally, he wants to triple-check for peace of mind. So, he asks God to perform the miracle once more, in reverse. Our long-suffering God delivers again: a dry fleece on dewy ground.

All those with Gideon prepare to fight. According to battle protocols, God culls Gideon's army by inviting anyone fearful to leave. More than two-thirds of the army say buh-bye. Then God issues another test for those who remain, leaving only three hundred who pass.

Knowing this young leader's tendency for skepticism and second-guessing, God provides a gift to solidify his resolve, sending Gideon a trusted servant to accompany him into the enemy camp to eavesdrop. They arrive just in time to overhear a Midianite warrior recounting to a friend a strange dream in which a loaf of barley bread tumbles into their camp and collapses an entire tent.

Gideon listens intently but can't understand. Then the enemy's friend provides the interpretation: God intends to give the small Israelite army a huge victory. In that yowzah moment, Gideon bows and worships. He returns to his troops and divides the paltry three hundred into three groups, equipping them with trumpets and empty jars containing lit torches—fine party favors for a sunset boat parade, but not war.

At the edge of the enemy camp, Gideon leads his troops to sound their horns, smash their clay jars, and raise their torches to the sky, shouting, "A sword for the LORD and for Gideon!" The half-asleep Midianites scream like middle schoolers in a haunted house and scramble away, but in the confusion of nighttime, they turn on each other. The Israelites seize the opportunity, rallying together. Their formidable enemy is defeated, and all who stand in the way or refuse to help are reduced to ruin.

God's Spirit wears Gideon like a garment.

In the wake of widespread victory, the Israelites beg Gideon to be their king. He will not hear of it, knowing there's only one true King. Even so, the Israelites enjoy peace throughout the land for forty years—all of Gideon's lifetime.

Indeed, God's Spirit wears Gideon like a garment.

> Our doubts and fears are no match for the Spirit of the Living God.

From Gideon's ongoing moments of doubt through the decisive victory, we are reminded that our doubts and fears, hesitancy and hang-ups, overthinking and second-guessing are no match for the Spirit of the Living God.

Here's the beauty: Clothes are shaped by those who wear them. When the Holy Spirit wears us, we are contoured by the *ruach*'s presence, formed by the Spirit's life in us. Just as Jesus said that a branch can't bear fruit by itself, a garment can't do anything by itself. Clothing is fully and wholly dependent on the One who wears it. Jesus promises the Holy Spirit to all his followers. If we are in Christ, we are both clothed in Christ and worn by the Holy Spirit who lives in us. The King of the Universe could choose to clothe himself in any splendor, yet God chooses us.

When I drove away from the Pensacola revival, I relished the freedom to choose whether to attend church. For months, I spent Sunday mornings sleeping in, brunching with friends, or hiking in the mountains. Then, one Sunday, I mustered the strength to visit a service. The moment the music began, I felt as if someone were pressing on a bruise. I wrapped my arms across my chest and rubbed my elbows to comfort myself, but every fiber of my being screamed to leave. I lasted less than twenty minutes.

In the parking lot, I sat alone in my car, gripping the steering wheel with white-knuckled intensity, taking measured breaths. A tidal wave of guilt crashed over me. My mind insisted that because I loved God, I should want to be at one of his meeting places, but my heart ached to be anywhere else. A part of me just couldn't be in church—at least not yet. I realized later that it was the same part of me that needed time to heal.

It's hard to tell people you're not going to church, especially when those people are pious Christians. They rarely understand. You instantly get lumped in with the reactionary rebels who are angry with the church, mad at God, or disinterested in the Divine.

I still loved God, prayed, read the Bible, and tried to process all that I had experienced. Yet whenever I neared a weekend service, all I felt was throbbing pain.

The Spirit is a healer, but healing often takes place over time rather than overnight. As the months rolled on, my heart grew tender, and the Spirit brought restoration. Six months later, I took a seat in the back of a church and felt relieved that it didn't hurt to be there. The next week, I showed up again. And then again. I found comfort and healing among this little liturgical community of believers who celebrated everything as a gift from the Father of Lights, in whom there is no shifting shadow.

We rarely heal in the same settings where we've been hurt.

I've come to understand that we rarely heal in the same settings where we've been hurt, and that's okay, despite any pressure from pious friends. I needed time to deprogram from the "do more, be more, accomplish more, and live as if everything depends on you" mindset, to rediscover the lavish love that never lets go, the grace that holds you tight no matter what, the joy of a Savior who bounces toddlers on his knees.

While my confidence in church as a gathering of believers had been restored, I remained skeptical of revivals. Then, more than two decades later, I heard rumors that the Spirit might be moving again in a town in rural Kentucky with a single stoplight. The community blessed by this outpouring of the Spirit diligently tried to sidestep the errors of other revivals. They were staving off the temptations to form a church, start a new institution, or stoke the fire so it could continue in perpetuity. *Could this be true?* I was skeptical. But there was only one way to find out.

By the time I arrived in Wilmore, Kentucky, on the campus of Asbury University, I had pieced together more of the details. Ten days before, the revival had sparked in an inauspicious way: A chapel speaker encouraged students to "become the love of God by experiencing the love of God."

Rather than rush to class when the chapel service ended, almost two dozen students lingered in spontaneous prayer and worship as a gentle peace filled the room. Other students and faculty soon caught wind, and the auditorium swelled with campus members. They stayed until the wee hours, praying and confessing, sharing Scripture and singing. The Holy Spirit hovered in a distinct way that couldn't be orchestrated by human hands. Word soon spread throughout the surrounding community, and within a few days, people were flying in from around the world.

When I arrived on campus, some sights were all too familiar: the lack of available parking, thick lines of people snaking around the campus, buses pulling into town. Parents with kids, students from other universities, and the elderly—people of every age and shape and size and background and ethnicity—had flocked to Wilmore, a town whose only franchise restaurant at the time was Subway.

I joined the back of the line that brisk February morning. I felt as nervous as a long-tailed cat in a room full of rockers. I kept touching my face, itching my torso, shifting from foot to foot. When I crossed the threshold into the auditorium, my shoulders relaxed. I was taken aback not by what I saw but by what I didn't see. The experience was markedly different from what I'd witnessed before. The gathering wasn't overly concerned with aesthetics and lacked many markers of the revival I'd been to in Florida: celebrity names, trendy songs leveraging emotion, flawless production. Asbury didn't even project lyrics onto a screen so worshipers could follow along. Instead, the stripped-down gathering radiated simplicity and devotion, centering on five elements:

1. Students leading Jesus-centered songs from every genre.

2. Students reading Scripture.

3. Students telling what Jesus was doing in their lives.

4. Prayer and confession for our broken lives and world.

5. An invitation to follow Jesus.

Rather than rely on the gravitas of personality or procedure, this heartfelt community centered on Christ. No one appeared to be grasping for power or platform. This open-handed gathering of believers understood that they had simply received a gift and were meant to share it with all who came.

The music, mostly dated and out of style, didn't aim for popularity. The diverse student-led worship teams chose well-worn hymns and time-tested choruses, some in Spanish or other languages. Yet the songs, the stories, the teaching, the prayers centered on Christ. Without a hint of "try harder and do more," the underlying message was "simply come and receive."

On my second day, when the line to the fifteen-hundred-person auditorium grew to more than half a mile, I opted for the overflow space across the street. Before the service started, people in the pews spontaneously stood up and read Scripture. A lone voice began singing and soon everyone joined in. A person in a back pew shared some wisdom, followed by another

Scripture. My hands cupped upward in a worshipful gesture. Nothing felt scripted, and gratitude hung in the air like cool morning mist over a serene lake.

Over the course of the weekend, I waited in lines next to powerful businesspeople and single moms struggling to pay next month's rent. I exchanged stories with people from denominations I'd never heard of and met Asbury alumni who had attended the school during a similar outpouring a half century prior. I encountered people who had come to know Christ during the Jesus Movement and even a few who remembered visiting Pensacola in the mid-1990s. Among the veteran believers, I sensed a spiritual hunger for a refreshing from the Holy Spirit, the God we need to know.

By the time I drove back to the airport, word had spread that the Holy Spirit's work at Asbury was already reaching to other college campuses.

Unlike at my previous experiences, the university leaders at Asbury seemed to recognize the importance of Christ's call for unity, "that they all may be one." Through prayer, they discerned that their purpose was not to build an expensive infrastructure to keep the outpouring going indefinitely. Nor did they veer from their founding mission as a Christian university, a commitment upheld for nearly a century and a half.

The Spirit's outpouring was freely given and freely given away. Just eighteen days after the revival began, the final service concluded. Thousands will attest that the sparks of the Holy Spirit ignited during those intense two and a half weeks at Asbury continue to burn bright in people's hearts and on university campuses worldwide.

Returning home after my weekend at Asbury, I felt drained from the travel but invigorated by the experience. The Spirit had delivered the final bit of healing my soul needed. A gentle grace restored me, like a supermoon appearing in the night sky, awakening my senses to the vastness of divine love.

When the Spirit moves in such emphatic bursts, human responses vary, sometimes flourishing and other times faltering. Yet we must remember that the Spirit isn't *something* we strive for but *Someone* who makes a home in us.

No matter what comes, may the Spirit wear us like a garment.

Breath Prayer

BREATHE IN:

Spirit of the Living God

BREATHE OUT:

Wear me like a garment.

SIX

THE SPIRIT WHO SPEAKS THROUGH US

STARING INTO THE MIRROR AFTER the most recent surgery, I looked like I'd stepped on a land mine. I felt like a hollow shell of my former self. The nurses had warned of the "cumulative" effects of cancer treatment, but I didn't know what that meant until I felt it in every fiber of my being. The body can only take so much.

A year of chemotherapy, dozens of rounds of radiation, and five surgeries had gnawed through my resilience and resolve. Now all we could do was wait to see if the aggressive cancer returned. Still in my thirties, I'd been thrust into an ongoing state of combat. I was fighting for top-notch medical care. Fighting for the fastest treatment. Fighting insurance companies and billing departments. Fighting medical blunders. Fighting infections. Fighting for my life. Even when the war was over, it felt like the battle had just begun. We had to rebuild our lives—and do so while living under the looming shadow of a recurrence.

This was no small feat. My body was frail and fatigued. My career needed resuscitating after being sidelined for medical procedures. My relationships needed rehabilitating as I struggled to navigate friendships with those who had disappeared after the diagnosis. My marriage needed mending as my husband, Leif, and I adjusted to a "new normal," and he was no longer my full-time caregiver. I fought to hold on to hope while I mourned all I had lost, realizing that life was never going back to how it had been before.

So when organizers for a large conference in Hawaii invited me to speak, I jumped at the opportunity. To my delight, the conference featured some unexpected and inspiring creative moments throughout. I noticed that during the worship sessions, an artist stood to the left of the stage and painted alongside as we sang. Some of the paintings were abstract, others more recognizable.

One morning I found myself captivated by the artist's careful brushstrokes. From what at first looked like random blotches emerged a powerful image: a faceless figure thrusting a long, silvery sword upward like a warrior. I blinked, then squinted, then blinked and squinted again. The portrait looked familiar.

Somewhere deep within, I sensed the Spirit whisper, *That's you.*

That's illogical, I protested.

Of course, it wasn't an actual portrait of me. It didn't have a face, and I'd never seen this artist before in my life. Plus, the convention center was packed with thousands of others facing their own trials. But I thought I understood what the Spirit was saying: It wasn't literally me, but it was metaphorically me. I saw myself in the imagery.

I'm sure I wasn't the only person seeing their struggles mirrored in the emerging image. Though our struggles differ, we all have warrior seasons. No one escapes this life unscathed. Sometimes we choose the battle, but more often, the battle chooses us. Sometimes the fight lasts only a brief moment; sometimes it spans years, even decades.

Maybe your battle began with a diagnosis, like mine, or with a traumatic injury. Perhaps you've had to stand over the grave of a loved one or feel the sharp pang every time you pass by an empty bedroom. Or maybe you're fighting the stinging disappointment that life didn't turn out like you'd expected. Maybe you have a broken marriage or no life partner at all, when you desperately wanted one. Whatever shape a battle takes, it can leave you exhausted, weary, an empty shell of your former self.

> The Spirit of God "shouts" in our pain because pain drowns out everything else.

C. S. Lewis once noted, "God whispers to us in our pleasures, speaks in our conscience, but shouts in our pain." I believe one of the reasons the Spirit of God "shouts" in our pain is because pain drowns out everything else. Battlefields are noisy by nature, and their decibel levels can reach thunderous heights. God shouts in our pain to cut through the uproar, ensuring we can hear his voice when we need it most.

As I gazed at the painting, a verse echoed loudly in my thoughts: "For the battle is not yours, but God's." Indeed, the Spirit of God can pierce through the loudest racket and ruckus in ways that steal our breath. Through the artist's familiar imagery, I was hearing the Spirit shout. But this was just the beginning of what the Spirit was up to that day.

The power of God's voice breaking through racket and ruckus traces back to the beginning of time. Spirit-infused words ignite during creation. With mere syllables, God hangs twinkly stars, spins the sun, twirls the moon, and hoists up the Alps. He fills the plains and floods the oceans with spiky, velvety, slithery, and scratchy creatures. Amid declarations of "Let there be . . . let there be . . . let there be" resounds the reverberating refrain, "It is good . . . it is good . . . it is very good." God could use anything—a wave of a hand, a tap of a finger, or a mere thought—as *une force de création*, yet he chooses to display his power and presence through spoken words.

As Scripture unfurls across soft vellum pages, we discover that God speaks with life-giving power to create the world and form humankind. Through words, God calls Moses and dispenses the Law atop Mount Sinai. Through history, prophecy, and poetry, the Spirit of the Living God even speaks *through humans* in ways that reveal God's power and presence. We discover that the Spirit can inhabit the syllables *we* speak.

As Israel transitions from the time of the judges to a monarchy, we meet a sparky lad named David, a tike born in the tiny town of Bethlehem—a place that becomes twice renowned a thousand years later with the birth of another king.

The youngest of eight sons, David is tasked with an assignment given to many children of that era—tending the sheep. Amid the thick solitude of the open desert, David fills his days writing lyrics in his head. He resists boredom by reaching into his worn leather pouch, removing one smooth stone after another, and fine-tuning his slingshot skills. Self-taught, David learns to defend his flock and himself from the fiercest of lions and the fastest of bears.

> The Spirit has David in hand, building in him the skills that will make him a servant king.

Whether slinging rocks or singing to sheep under the muted light of the Milky Way, little does David know that the Spirit has him in hand, building in him the skills that will make him a servant king, a great shepherd for the sheep of Israel, and "a man after God's own heart."

Then a prophet named Samuel comes to town and interrupts David's quiet, obscure existence. Searching for a king to replace Saul, the prophet first inspects all of David's brothers, but just as in Goldilocks's famous trespassing episode with the three bears, none of them is just right. But the moment Samuel lays eyes on David, the Lord tells him to get up and go: *This is the one!* Samuel opens a horn of olive oil and drizzles it atop David's head. The velvety liquid conditions David's hair, but this is more than a spa treatment: This is a holy anointing. And "the Spirit of the Lord rushed upon David from that day forward."

A few years earlier, when Samuel anointed Saul as Israel's first king, the Spirit of God had rushed upon Saul too. Sadly, the job went to Saul's head. Whenever God instructed him to do one thing, Saul invariably did the other.

Saul and David stand in stark contrast. Saul repeatedly attempts to kill David, but David refuses to kill Saul, even when given the chance. While both sin and rebel, Saul blames while David repents. Though neither is perfect, Saul rejects the Spirit's nudges and turns to dark arts. David, despite his personal failures, strives to live in tandem with the Spirit. Both men struggle toward the end of their lives, but the last words of David are an "inspired utterance." Reflecting on the Spirit's presence throughout his life, David says:

> The Spirit of the LORD spoke through me;
>   his word was on my tongue.

The Spirit of God breathes life into many of David's words, both spoken and written. A millennium or so later, Jesus affirms this when the Pharisees question his authority. Jesus quotes one of David's psalms, attesting that David was "speaking by the Spirit."

Spirit-empowered speech reaches far beyond the early kings of Israel. The Spirit speaks through Amasai, one of David's chief captains, prophesies through Moses and his seventy elders, and even inhabits the utterances of a gentile named Balaam.

When the Spirit wears Azariah like a garment, Azariah speaks urgently to David's great-great-grandson, Asa, the king of Judah. Azariah's words spark reform and repentance among the people of Judah and Jerusalem. The Spirit also rests on the lips of Jahaziel, infusing courage into Israelite troops: "Do not be afraid or discouraged because of this vast army. For the battle is not yours, but God's"—the very words the Spirit echoed to me during the worship service in Hawaii.

The Spirit Who Speaks Through Us

Those in the Old Testament whose speech is electrified by the Holy Spirit are sometimes called "prophets," but don't mistake them for fortune-tellers, soothsayers, or crystal-ball consultants. Prophets are *spokespeople for God,* and they include Deborah, Zechariah, Huldah, Isaiah, Ezekiel, and Micah. These spokespeople, among others, apply God's words to the situations before them, proclaim God's glory, call out human sin, and declare the redemption and hope God offers. Centuries later, the apostle Peter affirms that even in their humanity, these prophets "spoke from God as they were carried along by the Holy Spirit."

> Prophets are spokespeople for God.

Spirit-led words flutter around Christ's earthly arrival like fireflies at dusk. When Elizabeth receives a visit from her cousin, she's filled with the Spirit, and sure enough, the Spirit infuses her words as she speaks about Mary and her child.

Prophetic syllables soon rest on Mary's tongue in the form of song. Then Elizabeth's husband, Zechariah, also filled with the Spirit, speaks of the history of God's people and the promise of their bright future. Even Elizabeth and Zechariah's son, John the Baptist, is filled with the Spirit prenatally and spends his life calling everyone within earshot to turn back to God.

When God speaks humanity into existence, he embeds life-giving speech within us. Proverbs paints a stunning landscape of what's possible:

> The mouth of the righteous is a fountain of life.
> The tongue of the wise brings healing.
> The lips of the righteous nourish many.

As followers of Jesus, we receive the gift of the Holy Spirit and have access to the same Spirit who inspired David and has been delivering words of life to the world since the dawn of creation. We have opportunities to speak life everywhere we go—to submit our hearts and minds and tongues to the Spirit and ask God to give us words to strengthen the weary and fortify the disheartened. Through the Spirit, we can utter care-filled words rather than careless ones. We can speak words that foster life rather than echo death. We can impart hope to those facing despair. We can ask the Spirit to help us call out gifts and talents in others that they may not even realize they possess.

> Through the Spirit, we can speak words that foster life.

How do we align with the Holy Spirit so that our words reflect the glory of Christ into which we are growing? One simple way is to marinate in the greatest love letter of all time—the Bible.

The Spirit of the Living God infuses power into the pages of this holy book. Scripture is "God-breathed," meaning you'll find the Spirit hovering above and nestled into the words of those who have documented the law, recorded the history, penned the psalms, and collected the proverbs. Through God's Word we discover our true selves and are molded and fashioned for every good, God-given task under the sun.

When we make space for the words of God to come alive in our hearts, they unleash an unmistakable transforming power in our attitudes and actions, shifting the way we see and speak to others. As we spend time with the Scriptures, we expand the library from which the Holy Spirit can draw in our lives.

If I sense the Spirit nudging me to say something to someone,

The Spirit Who Speaks Through Us

I often struggle: *Is this from the Spirit? When should I speak the words? How should I speak them? And what tone should I use?*

Much like when sorting through dreams, we must start by using Scripture to scrutinize any words we suspect are prompted by the Spirit. If the syllables are Spirit-given, then they'll never conflict with Scripture or the character of God. And even when the words are aligned with both, the discernment process has just begun. We must also check our hearts to ensure that our speech and the tone we use reflect the compassion and love of God.

If we're uncertain in any way—about the person, the timing, or the words themselves—it's best to take time to pray and wait. It's wiser to err on the side of silence paired with extended prayer than to speak rashly.

I've also found that words given by the Spirit are meant to be a gift. Just as we'd never want a gift-giver to say, "This is your gift, and you must like it!," we must approach others with a dogged humility that honors them above ourselves. We should resist the urge to strong-arm or take a "thus saith the Lord" approach. The outcome of the words we speak depends on the work of the Spirit, not on ourselves or our persuasiveness. The Spirit will use our efforts, however imperfect, to convey to the recipients what needs to be known. Knowing this, we can lead with a gentleness that stoops low with humility, saying, "This may be of no use to you at all, but I just sense in my heart that . . ." or "I've been praying for you, and this may not mean anything, but this came to mind . . ." This kind of framing leaves room to acknowledge that we sense the Spirit imperfectly, and sometimes the words on our lips are just our own.

One chapter of the Bible that helps guide me in the discernment process is nestled in an ancient letter written by Paul. First Corinthians 12 explores spiritual gifts and how they work together among God's people, particularly involving speech. The next chapter begins:

> If I speak in the tongues of men or of angels, but do not have love, *I am only a resounding gong or a clanging cymbal.* If I have the gift of prophecy and can fathom all mysteries and all knowledge, and if I have a faith that can move mountains, but do not have love, *I am nothing.* If I give all I possess to the poor and give over my body to hardship that I may boast, but do not have love, *I gain nothing.*

When our mouths are consecrated by the Spirit, when our words are submitted to the Spirit, each syllable will be infused with love. We can sift our words through 1 Corinthians 13 like a colander to see what, if anything, remains.

If your words are always patient, always kind, always protecting, always hoping, always persevering, you can have a measure of confidence the Spirit is at work. If your words are devoid of arrogance and pride, dishonor and self-centeredness, anger and grudges, the Spirit may be operating through them. If your words refuse to delight in evil and instead rejoice with truth, there could be a touch of the Spirit in what you say. And if your words are marked by faith, hope, and love most of all, the Spirit just might be resting on your lips. Spirit-infused words have a shelf life beyond that of all the ordinary syllables we speak.

Just as the Spirit has infused the words of those who came

before you, the *ruach* wants to infuse your words so they drip with the power, presence, and purposes of God.

Back in Hawaii, as we sang the final chorus, I watched intently as the artist added the final brushstrokes to the image of the faceless figure holding the sword. The Spirit continued to echo, *That's you.* The more I stared at the painting, the more I felt connected to the imagery. After everyone was dismissed from the session, I gingerly approached the artist to compliment him on his work. "I really like your painting of the warrior," I said.

"That picture is you," he said.

"Wha . . . what?" I stammered.

"I sensed there's a message the Spirit wants to give you," he said.

My mouth fell agape as he pulled out a folded piece of white notebook paper with a note scribbled in thick black marker. Then he read the words he sensed the Spirit had said:

> I know that there is no one that loves
> your life, heart, mind, soul
> more than the One who formed it.
> You have always been the one I've fought for.
> Let go of the sword you hold, and rest.
> I am so proud of you.

As he pressed the note into my palm, tears streamed down my sun-kissed cheeks. The Spirit had spoken the truth—the portrait *was* me—through this artist. Until then, I hadn't fully acknowledged how hard and long the battle had been. I hadn't realized the toll the medical treatments had taken on my body. I'd been trying to outrun the pain, outmaneuver the loss, outsmart the odds that the disease might return with a vengeance. I'd fought hard to survive and strained to remember my bygone life.

The Spirit used the artist's words to deliver a message I desperately needed: It was time to put down my sword. I didn't have to fight on my own. God was fighting on my behalf. The Spirit was waiting to embrace me in ways I'd never known. All I needed to do was loosen my grip and trust the One who loved me beyond measure.

It's time to put down your sword.

When Leif and I arrived home, I put down my sword. I discovered the Spirit nudging me to trust—to trust the *ruach* to renew friendships, to refresh my marriage, to strengthen us for the next medical challenge we would inevitably face. Life never reverted to the way it was before cancer. But through the grieving and healing, I discovered that Christ makes new life possible, and wells of compassion flooded my heart that I wouldn't have known otherwise.

Maybe you know a thing or two about feeling battle-weary. You may see physical scars when you glance in the mirror, or maybe your scars are emotional or spiritual—the ones that come from trying to reach an estranged child or care for an aging parent with whom you've had a complicated relationship. Perhaps you carry the marks from unspeakable physical or emotional abuse. Or the scars left in the wake of speaking up for truth at work when something wasn't right or fair.

Maybe for you, too, the Spirit is prompting you to put down your sword.

I don't know where I'd be if that artist hadn't delivered those words to me on that day. The Spirit is faithful, and I'm confident that other images, Scriptures, people, or words would have been used to guide my heart back. But I'm so grateful the artist—whose name I still don't know—allowed the Spirit to rest on his lips.

And how might your world transform if you let the Spirit rest on yours?

 Breath Prayer

BREATHE IN:

Spirit of the Living God

BREATHE OUT:

Be ever on my lips.

SEVEN

THE SPIRIT WHO WORKS IN THE WAITING

NEITHER MY MOM NOR MY DAD is good at staying in one place.

At the tender age of two, my parents took me to a waterfront restaurant in South Florida, where we watched the boats glide by. On a whim, they decided to take up sailing. Within a week, they called a broker and purchased a vessel in New Jersey. They soon embarked out of New York Harbor for the Bahamas without the foggiest idea how to operate the boat they now trusted with their lives and mine. Somehow, we successfully navigated the thousand-mile journey from New England to the Bahamas, making a pit stop along the way to enroll me in swim lessons in case I fell overboard.

The expedition became an adventure of a lifetime, complete with breathtaking sunsets, lobster dinners, and wildly colorful underwater reefs. But the trip also included mechanical problems, dangerous waterspouts, and running aground. Despite the challenges, sailing became a central part of our family life.

We returned to the Bahamas many times throughout my childhood. When I was eight, Mom decided I'd spend all of third grade living at sea. So she enrolled me in a homeschool program long before homeschooling was considered a reputable form of education. I discovered that if I completed all my schoolwork in one day, I could spend the other six swimming, diving, and exploring. I learned to spear lobster and gather conch. In the late afternoons I caught grunt fish, which I cleaned, cooked, and served to our dog, Puppy, whom I had named when I was four.

Over the years, my parents owned various vessels, including a trawler, trimaran, catamaran, and various single hulls. Sometime in my thirties, while Leif and I were living in Colorado, they shared with us that they had decided to try living on land again. A new development had opened in the Abaco Islands in the northern Bahamas, and one of Dad's friends said, "You've gotta look at the property!"

So they sailed off to the remote island of Tilloo Cay, where only two other houses existed and sat empty for much of the year. The island lacked running water, electricity, or a paved road. A single overgrown path cut across the island for almost half a mile—the perfect place, I'd later discover, to accumulate endless bug bites. The island's only sandy beach was nicknamed "Junk Beach" due to the mounds of trash that washed ashore each day.

Despite all this, my parents fell in love with the property. They hired a builder to design and construct a studio cottage they could live in until the day they could build a larger home. They had been assured that electricity would be installed on the island within two months. Meanwhile, they would live on their trawler anchored offshore.

"We gave the builder a huge deposit, and soon all the materials we needed to build the cottage arrived on our rock," Mom recently recounted to me. "But then the 2007 real estate market crash happened, and the builder disappeared."

"Couldn't you hire someone else?" I asked.

"The island was so remote," she said, "there was no one to call. We asked everyone if they knew someone, but there was no one."

They prayed and prayed, but no one came. Worse, they had a huge investment of building materials sitting on the property. A huge storm rolled in, and heavy winds blew salt water atop their supplies. Bags of cement hardened. Wooden doors swelled. Nails rusted. They remained aboard their trawler and prayed that help would come.

Sooner or later, all of us find ourselves in situations that are just too much, when the life we knew or envisioned collapses, the place we considered home becomes uninhabitable, the dreams we once held dear are crushed. When we think it can't get worse, it does. We wake up and realize we lack the resources, connections, and know-how to pull ourselves up by our bootstraps and push through.

All we can do is pray. And wait.

The Israelites knew this feeling too. They'd spent years living in excruciating exile, displaced from their home. They longed for God to answer their cries, scoop them up, and return them to their homeland. They prayed and waited, yet God remained silent.

One notable trait of Old Testament prophets: a resistance to their calling. They never seem to race to the "Now Hiring Prophets" booth at the holy job fair and beg, "*Please, please* let me be the super weirdo around town who performs bizarre acts, makes people uncomfortable, and delivers mostly terrible news."

Case in point: When Moses is tapped to talk to Pharaoh about the future, he stutters that he's not cut out for public speaking. When Jeremiah discovers that God ordained him to be a prophet in the womb, he argues that he's far too young. And when Isaiah receives his assignment, he protests, essentially whining, "But how long do I have to do this?"

Ezekiel is no exception.

During the first wave of attacks on Jerusalem led by Nebuchadnezzar in 597 BCE, Ezekiel, among a slew of other Jewish prisoners, is kidnapped and imprisoned in a camp. Five years later, still stuck in the squalor, Ezekiel turns thirty. The day called for an epic celebration surrounding his installation as a priest to serve in the temple, but it turns out to be a birthday to forget.

Amid deep disappointment, the Spirit ignites Ezekiel's imagination with images of storm clouds, mysterious creatures, and spinning wheels within wheels—conveying that God's presence isn't limited to the ark of the covenant: God lives in a mobile home, or rather, a mobile throne.

When Ezekiel drops face down, the Spirit lifts him to his feet and appoints him as a holy mouthpiece. The Spirit warns him not to get his hopes up, for most days his words will fall on deaf ears. The prophet soon feels the deep distress of his calling.

Ezekiel uses everything from spoken words to street theater to garner the people's attention and deliver the Spirit's messages. He builds a model of Jerusalem and stages an attack. He shaves off his hair and dices it with a sword like he's a theatrical chef at a hibachi restaurant. He plays the role of the fuzzy scapegoat on the Day of Atonement. He even lies on his side for an entire year—call the chiropractor!—and eats food that tastes like smoked dung as a sign of what's to come.

All the prophet's warnings come true. Jerusalem falls. The temple everyone hoped to return to is destroyed. The false prophets are purged. In the wake of the catastrophe and chaos, it looks like all is lost. But, as we have learned from the Spirit hovering over chaotic waters, that's when the Spirit of God does something surprising and delightful.

Though God may have abandoned his temple, he hasn't abandoned his people. There's a future beyond captivity and a hope for Israel, for all nations, and even for all of creation. A new king will rise who will be like no other.

> The Spirit of the Living God rekindles hope among a discouraged Israel.

The Spirit of the Living God rekindles hope among a discouraged Israel, lifts Ezekiel through a vision, and plops him down in a bone-strewn valley. The landscape likely makes Ezekiel queasy, as these are *human* bones and touching them serves as a fast pass to becoming unclean. Skulls and scapulas. Vertebrae and ribs. Femurs and phalanges. Shoulder blades and tailbones as far as the eye can see.

"Can these bones live?" the Lord asks.

Unsure of how to respond, Ezekiel confesses, "Only God knows." I suspect the Lord takes pleasure in the prophet's humble response, because he invites Ezekiel into the process of speaking life into this graveyard. Ezekiel closes his eyes and prophesies. Not once, but twice, the Lord declares to the bones that when *ruach* is in you, then you will come to life. The gripping scene continues:

> And as I was prophesying, there was a noise,
> a rattling sound, and the bones came together,
> bone to bone. I looked, and tendons and
> flesh appeared on them and skin covered
> them, but there was no *ruach* in them.

To envision this, lean in and listen. Barely a shadow can be made out in the near pitch darkness. Ezekiel paces through the bone-strewn alley, following the Lord across the valley floor. The dry, white, sun-bleached skeletons are the only objects bright enough to reflect the dim light. The Lord commands Ezekiel to prophesy to the bones. Ezekiel doesn't flinch; he simply obeys. The guttural syllables echoing off the surrounding hills are soon joined by a soft rustle that grows into a steady shuffling—before, behind, all around Ezekiel.

Close your eyes and listen as the words are punctuated by the bang of hard objects clacking against one another. Ezekiel's words are drowned out as the constant rattle rises to a raucous clamor. "Then you will know that I am the Lord," Ezekiel pronounces into the storm of noise. He looks on as the valley fills with thwacking—no, snapping—as if tens of thousands of workers are slapping mortar on bricks throughout the valley. Then, a mysterious rush like tens of thousands of tent lashes being tightened in a camp. Next, dead silence. Before Ezekiel's eyes, these thwacking and stretching tendons and flesh appear on the assembled bones. The sequence is no accident.

Anyone who has witnessed the slaughter of an animal, whether in antiquity or today, understands this order is the reversal of the decomposition process.

It's as if God has hit the rewind button, not in an instant but in phases—a reminder that coming back to life takes time. Whether it takes three days or fifty days or four hundred years, you can't rush a resurrection—let alone predict how long it will take. The prophet stands before the dead bones and observes, "There was no *ruach* in them."

The Lord commands Ezekiel:

> "Prophesy to the *ruach*; prophesy, son of man, and
> say to it, 'This is what the Sovereign Lord says:
> Come, *ruach*, from the four *ruach* and *ruach* into
> these slain, that they may live.'" So I prophesied as
> he commanded me, and *ruach* entered them; they
> came to life and stood up on their feet—a vast army.

Ezekiel obeys and the Spirit breathes life. Diaphragms rise and descend. Coughs release at the flood of oxygen. Gleaming sparkles light up eyes. Fingers and toes wiggle. Torsos rise. Imagine smiles sweeping across faces. Gusty laughter breaking free.

Through this vision, the Spirit reveals to the prophet and to us that life comes from the Spirit and is also restored by the Spirit. Beyond the veil of impossibility, the Spirit breathes life into barren places and resurrects hope from the ashes. Even in the darkest nights, the work of *ruach* continues, weaving threads of redemption into the fabric of existence. Not even death can halt the purposes of God.

The apostle Paul echoes this refrain centuries later when he declares:

> *The Spirit of God*, who raised Jesus from the dead,
> lives in you. And just as God raised Christ Jesus
> from the dead, he will give life to your mortal
> bodies by this *same Spirit* living within you.

Notice how *ruach* works among the lifeless. The return to life isn't accomplished in a single action or movement. The Spirit's work unfolds over time, rather than in an instant. The *ruach* moves through the in-between at a sacred pace through this sacred space. And often we are required to wait.

> The Spirit's work often unfolds over time, rather than in an instant.

Maybe you're waiting for something right now. Maybe you're waiting for your child to come to faith—or return to it. Or you're waiting to meet that special someone who will become your spouse. Maybe you're waiting for the job that can help you pay rent. Or for the test results to reveal the next steps. Or you're waiting for a house to sell or to be built.

It's easy to get impatient, to lose hope. We don't like to wait. We want God to work *pronto!*, in the way we expect, using the means we expect, on the timeline we expect. But the Spirit of the Living God works through stages, carefully and purposefully bringing about new life over time. When we begin to recognize that provision and grace and healing often come in stages, our hope will expand.

Remember this: Just because you don't see something happening doesn't mean the Spirit isn't working in the waiting.

Mom and Dad continued to pray and ask anyone and everyone for help. Still, no one came. But among the building supplies on their overgrown property, they found a single book from Home Depot about how to frame a house.

"Your dad looked at it and said, 'This is just beyond us,'" Mom told me. "So I encouraged him to go through only one chapter at a time. We couldn't peek at chapter 2 until we finished chapter 1. We had to take it step by step."

When the weather cleared and the water calmed, my parents puttered the twelve-mile round trip to Marsh Harbour in their dinghy to visit the hardware store. They filled their tiny boat with as many new supplies as it could hold without sinking, making multiple trips back and forth to their property. The pile of hammers, machetes, saws, shovels, and an assortment of power tools stacked high. Despite what had become years of repeated promises from the Bahamian government, electricity still wasn't being installed.

Mom and Dad prayed and waited. Days slipped into weeks. When no one came, my sixtysomething parents resolved to clear the lot themselves. After weeks of machete swinging, their hands were blistered, and their skin bubbled with bites from mosquitoes and no-see-ums. My mom unwittingly cleared poisonwood trees, leaving her covered in cherry-red, swollen, watery sores from head to toe.

While my mom's body healed, my parents continued to pray for help. But no one came. So they dug deep holes for the pilings, the supports for the cottage. When their shovels hit rock, the only way forward was to purchase a generator and rent a jackhammer, so that's exactly what they did. My father jiggled like Jell-O and dripped like a faucet in the humid, ninety-five-degree heat. They again prayed for help. Still, no one came.

They traveled back to town to buy bags of cement. Dad mixed them to set the pilings. The second chapter of the book showed them how to connect floor joists and plywood. The next chapter helped them construct the walls.

Trouble arose when they reached chapter 4 on building rafters.

"Those are tricky," Mom recalled. "Every cut had to be precise, and the book wasn't specific enough. We said, 'Lord, we're in trouble, and we don't know what to do next.'"

They prayed and waited. Meanwhile, the pressure to complete the home intensified. Hurricane season was less than five months away. If they didn't finish in time, a rogue storm could destroy everything they had swatted, sweated, hammered, and jackhammered to accomplish.

My parents continued to pray and wait. They'd nearly given up hope when a gentleman who had purchased another lot on the island stopped by to introduce himself. The man happened to be a builder from Massachusetts and knew how to cut rafters. The kind stranger cut one perfect rafter that became the template for the rest.

Next came the roof, but Mom couldn't lift the heavy sheets of plywood fifteen feet up the ladder to Dad. They prayed again, and still no one came.

Then one morning a man from Haiti wandered down the path. He could barely speak English but gestured enough to communicate: "You have work?" Nelson became the helping hands my parents needed. Each morning, he caught a ride on a speedboat from Marsh Harbour that ferried tourists out to farther islands. My parents learned a few Haitian Creole words from Nelson, and he learned a few words of English from them. Each day, they fed him a big meal, and soon Nelson felt like family. My parents asked me to track down a Haitian Creole Bible for Nelson, and they told me how his eyes lit up when he received it.

Even with Nelson's strength, the challenges continued. The cottage's height made climbing dangerous, and the book didn't include a chapter on how to build stairs. My parents prayed again, "Lord, we need someone who can help—please send them fast."

Later that month, someone wandered down the path looking

for a friend who lived on the same island. They chatted for a while before Dad asked, "You don't know how to build stairs, do you?"

"Yeah, I've been a carpenter and woodworker for years," he said. The stranger stayed late into the afternoon teaching my dad how to construct stairs.

"That's how we got safely to the main floor," my mom explained. "Without him, we really could have hurt ourselves."

Most of the original building supplies left on the property from my parents' initial order were exactly what they needed and were surprisingly in good condition.

"One of the odd things was that they sent far too many stainless-steel hurricane ties," Mom recalled. "When Nelson and I were tying the walls to the flooring and fastening everything together, I thought, *Why not use them all?* So we did."

With hurricane season hurtling toward them, Dad, Mom, and Nelson worked tirelessly, seven days a week, ten hours a day. They finally reached the point where they could hang the fiber cement siding on the exterior. After installing the windows, Dad recognized a huge miscalculation he'd made. Feeling defeated, he had to remove all the glass and start again, losing precious time.

"Basically, that's how it went," Mom said. "Sometimes we'd just have to rip out what we'd done and start again."

The time pressure was excruciating. Whenever they lacked a screw or bolt or fitting, they had to wait for good weather to make the twelve-mile round trip to the hardware store, where every employee knew them by name.

"Word soon spread in our part of the Abacos that two old people were trying to build a house, and you ought to go over and see because it's really funny," my mom said.

Locals started to stop by on a regular basis to see the spectacle for themselves. One day, a curious visitor suggested making the space beneath the main floor into a bedroom and bathroom. Even with seven-foot ceilings, it was a great idea. That's how the studio cottage became a one-bedroom, two-bath home. Another visitor just happened to have a manual on building cabinets and offered to rent out his basic woodworking tools. My dad handcrafted the bathroom, kitchen, and closet cabinets.

"We'd hit obstacles, and then people would show up with the training or skills or talents we needed. This went from simply building a house to a journey of faith."

My parents had been faced with a pile of disassembled, seawater-soaked, sun-dried building supplies, just as Ezekiel had faced a valley of dry, sun-bleached bones. And just like the oddball prophet, they experienced the gradual, unfolding work of the Spirit making something marvelous out of what looked like a total loss—and preparing them to withstand any coming storms.

As my parents were completing the final touches on the house, Nelson disappeared without warning. A day passed, then two, and a week later, my parents worried that something bad might have happened. Then the next month, my mom received a call from Nelson. He had made it to the United States and needed his final payment.

> You can experience the gradual, unfolding work of the Spirit making something marvelous out of what looks like a total loss.

"We were able to get him the funds and some extra so he could start his new life," Mom said.

Many months after clearing their lot on a remote, buggy island, my parents completed their cottage—just in time for hurricane season. The experience convinced them to never build the main house.

They bought tanks to collect rainwater for bathing and washing. They ran their generator an hour a day for basics like turning on the microwave or flushing the toilet. At night, they used a twelve-volt battery in the bedroom to run a single light and two mini fans. They lived on the premises for two years before the Bahamian government finally fulfilled its promise to install electricity on the island. And all the woodworking and building skills they picked up along the way were later used to help others on the surrounding islands with repairs and projects.

Meanwhile, my parents developed deep friendships with people who lived on nearby islands. They planted papaya and banana trees and fished from their dock. The island became a place where they could flourish. Eight years later, though, they sensed a stirring in their hearts, uncertain whether to stay or go.

Once again, they prayed and asked the Spirit to guide them. Mom stenciled a "For Sale" sign and nailed it to one of their dock's pilings. Instead of contacting a Realtor or advertising the home in Marsh Harbour, they simply prayed and waited.

"If we're supposed to move, bring us a buyer, Lord," they petitioned.

Within a week, their immediate neighbor came by and said he wanted to purchase their property. The offer allowed them to break even during a softening in the real estate market. The day the sale closed, they celebrated.

The next day, I called my mom.

"Test results are back," I choked out, tears welling up. "I have cancer."

The timing of the sale was ideal for my parents to return to Colorado to be nearby during my treatment. We prayed for a place for them to stay since they didn't own a home, and quite miraculously, our neighbors needed a long-term dog sitter. My parents were close by for some of the most excruciating days of my life. And I for theirs.

Ninety days after I was diagnosed, my father was diagnosed with cancer too. We found ourselves praying and waiting, battling the vicious disease side by side.

That was more than a decade ago.

As of our most recent scans and tests, neither my dad nor I have any evidence of cancer. Now in their eighties, my parents have returned to living on a boat in the Bahamas and plan to do so for as long as the Spirit gives them breath.

When you find yourself wandering in the valley of the shadow of death, when you feel drained of life and empty of breath, do not lose hope. When prayer for the impossible is all that's left, embrace it fully. While we may not always receive the answers we hope for or on the timeline we long for, we can know that our petitions never go unheard. We can trust that the Spirit is working while we are waiting—building in and through our lives a home that can withstand any coming storm.

Oh, and as far as those extra stainless-steel hurricane ties that "just happened" to come with the building supplies? A dozen years later, Hurricane Dorian wrought unspeakable destruction throughout the Abacos. All the homes surrounding the one my parents constructed were destroyed. The one built by the two old people remained standing. The only thing the house lost was a single shutter.

 Breath Prayer

BREATHE IN:

Spirit of the Living God

BREATHE OUT:

Sustain me while I wait.

EIGHT

THE SPIRIT WHO WASTES NOTHING

THE POLICE CRUISERS' SIRENS WAILED throughout the cemetery, drawing the attention of a few passersby who paused near the entrance, straining their necks to see what had brought the emergency vehicles. Frantic officers crisscrossed among headstones searching for something. But what?

An unassuming businessman, my friend Phil had chosen that day to visit an old graveyard in Albany, New York. He was in town for meetings, which provided the perfect excuse for a passionate history buff like him to fulfill a personal goal: to visit the burial place of America's twenty-first president, Chester Arthur, along with the graves of several Supreme Court justices.

Phil was standing near President Arthur's grave when the

chaos descended, leaving him spooked. He stood motionless as he watched police officers comb row after row of the dearly departed as emergency vehicles whizzed by. A cemetery population isn't prone to emergencies, of course, and Phil was growing uneasy. *Was a criminal on the loose, hiding among the tombstones?* he wondered.

Just then, one of the police vehicles ground to a stop beside Phil's car. "Have you seen anything or anyone around here?" the officer asked.

"No, sir," Phil replied. "What's all this commotion about?"

"We're looking for a child," the officer responded. "We got a call that a large headstone collapsed on a boy while he was playing. The grandmother is on her cell phone in a panic, unable to help the child, but we can't locate them, and the caretaker is nowhere to be found."

The vast cemetery spanned more than 450 acres of thick woods and rolling hills that were threaded with streams. Amid thirty-five miles of twisty roads and nearly one hundred thousand graves, trying to find the boy felt like searching for a heartbeat in an abandoned city.

"Sir, do you mind if I ask what section the grandmother called from?" Phil asked.

"I think it was in the teens—maybe fifteen, sixteen, or seventeen," he replied.

Phil nodded in the direction the emergency crews were heading. "They're not going to find the boy there. If you want to find the boy, you've got to go down *that* road," Phil said, pointing. "You'll find him on the left-hand side."

"Do you live near here?" the officer asked.

"No, sir, I'm from Alabama. I've never been to this cemetery in my life," Phil said. "But I promise you, if you head that way, you'll find them."

The officer climbed into his vehicle and sped in the direction Phil had indicated. He radioed the other emergency vehicles, and they soon followed. Once all the vehicles passed, Phil followed them at a safe distance. Cresting a hill, Phil spotted the panicking grandmother. The emergency crew worked together to lift the tombstone and free the child.

When Phil walked into the cemetery that day, little did he know that the Spirit had prepared him for just this moment. Isn't that just like the Spirit? He's always using the right people with the right knowledge at the right time in the right way to bring forth life, even in places of death and decay.

Growing up, I loved the adventures of the Hebrew prophet Daniel and his friends. It seemed like they were always finding themselves trapped in another escape room. Whether engulfed in a blazing furnace or chilling in a den full of lions, they kept making miraculous exits with mere moments to spare.

As I grew older, I gleaned the more practical takeaways from their escapades: the importance of trusting God, growing in faith, and living in rhythms of obedience. But I never heard anyone highlight the work of the Holy Spirit in these stories. The Old Testament book that bears Daniel's name is steeped in miracle upon miracle, yet somehow the pagan king Nebuchadnezzar noticed the work of the Spirit long before I did.

On our road to Pentecost, we enter a new era in Israel's history—God's people are living in exile. That's when we meet Nebuchadnezzar, who ranks among the worst villains in the Hebrew Bible. Scripture doesn't tell us anything about the ruler's childhood, but I sometimes wonder when little Nebby's mother first noticed her child's cruel streak. Perhaps it was when his siblings let out bloodcurdling screams, or when a string of servants started showing up for work with missing fingers, or when the family pets met sudden deaths or mysteriously vanished.

By the time we meet Nebuchadnezzar, he's become famous for torturing, terrorizing, and taking life. In one episode that would make a riveting true crime podcast, King Zedekiah of Judah makes an agreement with King Nebuchadnezzar to stave off additional bloodshed, then breaks the treaty. Rather than issue a diplomatic warning or swift military response, King Nebuchadnezzar hatches a plan of utmost cruelty.

First, he sends his Babylonian army to camp outside Jerusalem and build a wall around it. After months of sleepless, anxiety-riddled nights spent wondering when the city will be attacked, King Zedekiah realizes the assault has already come, as the last crates of food and supplies dwindle to nothing. The Babylonian army waits until the people waste away to hollow frames of skin and bone before breaking through the city walls. King Zedekiah and his weakened soldiers attempt to flee to the Jordan Valley, but the Babylonian army chases them down and captures poor Zedekiah.

Granting Zedekiah a quick death would have been far too kind for the bloodthirsty King Nebuchadnezzar, who finds great pleasure in dragging Zedekiah's sons before him. One by one, he butchers them with gruesome instruments until the final, haunting scream. Then Zedekiah's eyes are punched out, so his sons' deaths are the last thing he sees.

Whatever psychological diagnosis you're tempted to assign King Nebuchadnezzar, you'd never, ever want him as a boss. But after the Babylonian army conquers Jerusalem, they look for attractive, healthy, well-educated quick learners to serve in the king's palace. That's when a foursome known as Daniel, Hananiah, Mishael, and Azariah are selected.

These palace refugees are thrust into a PhD program on Babylonian culture. Syllable by syllable, they learn the language, perfecting verb tenses and pronunciations. They stay up until the wee hours memorizing history and folklore for pesky pop quizzes. They even receive Babylonian names: Daniel becomes Belteshazzar, Hananiah becomes Shadrach, Mishael becomes Meshach, and Azariah becomes Abednego.

Somewhere along the way, they realize they're not being educated; they're being indoctrinated. The whole program was designed to strip away their most precious commodity—their identity as children of Israel's one true God. Like the children in C. S. Lewis's Narnia, the longer they remain in this foreign land, the harder it becomes to remember their true home.

The foursome draws a line by asking for one exemption from

the program requirements. Some of the king's food isn't kosher, meaning it fails to meet Jewish dietary laws. Worse, the king's plenty is gained through injustice, lack of mercy, and cruelty to the poor. This original God Squad asks to substitute basic veggies and water for the king's rich, calorie-dense tasting menu. Their academic advisor grants the request, and ten days after adopting their diet of vegetables and water, the foursome actually *gains* weight.

Following this expression of dogged obedience, a divine gift descends:

> God *gave* these four young men *knowledge*
> and *understanding* in *every* kind of literature
> and *wisdom*. Daniel also understood
> visions and dreams of *every* kind.

Rather than remove the foursome *from* their circumstances, God meets them *in* their circumstances. Together, they receive *exceedingly more* of what they'll need, not just for that moment but for what is to come.

> The Spirit doesn't waste anything.

These spiritual gifts aren't brand spanking new to the four young men. Remember, they were initially selected because they're "suitable for instruction in all wisdom, knowledgeable, perceptive, and capable." The Spirit *enhances* the gifts already placed within them. The Spirit doesn't waste anything.

This spiritual enrichment becomes impossible to miss. When the king examines the young nobles three years into their training, Daniel and his friends are the superstar candidates:

The Spirit Who Wastes Nothing

In every matter of *wisdom* and *understanding*
about which the king questioned them, he found
them *ten times better* than all the magicians
and enchanters in his whole kingdom.

The king appoints them to his court, establishing Daniel as governor of Babylon with Shadrach, Meshach, and Abednego serving alongside him. And the timing could not have been more perfect.

One night, the king, who has been a nightmare to others, has a nightmare himself. The dream begins peaceably enough, with a towering tree reaching toward the stars, laden with fruit. Under its shady leaves, creatures of every size and sort find shelter and nourishment. Then, in the dream, a holy messenger prophesies that the branches will be hacked off, the leaves stripped, and the trunk reduced to a stub. The mangled stump will morph into a wild beast and roam among the animals of the field and sun-cured grass of the earth.

Nebuchadnezzar sits bolt upright in bed, tight-chested, gasping for air, grateful to still be alive. Overwhelmed with dread, he summons his band of Babylonian wise men—a lineup of sorcerers, conjurers, astrologers, and diviners versed in the dark arts. Gathering at the palace, they each take a turn at interpreting the king's frightful dream.

But all the king's horses and all the king's men can't interpret the dream or make Nebuchadnezzar feel better again. That is, except for one. God's supernatural wisdom and understanding empower Daniel to interpret *every* vision and dream.

I wonder if Daniel paused to gulp a breath before speaking,

since the king had never been one to take bad news well. Daniel explains that the tree represents the king, who is about to lose everything, including his sanity. Just as God can make losers into leaders, God is about to make this leader into a loser.

Daniel begs the king to accept his advice: Dump your shares in evil and invest in all that is good. Replace your cruelty with compassion and show mercy to all.

Even a pagan king like Nebuchadnezzar can see what's going on here. Three times, he recognizes the Spirit in Daniel:

> The *ruach* of the holy gods is in him.
> I know that the *ruach* of the holy gods is in you.
> The *ruach* of the holy gods is in you.

Raised in a culture steeped in many gods, Nebuchadnezzar hasn't yet grasped the full reality of the one true God when he makes these observations. But his repeated acknowledgments reveal he recognizes the Spirit of God working within Daniel. Yet Nebuchadnezzar remains far too sure of himself to heed anyone else's advice—even when he asks for it. Months later, he's still so self-centered that he describes Babylon as the place "*I* have built" with "*my* mighty power" and for "*my* majesty."

Sooner or later, self-absorption brings out the worst in all of us. Surrounded by "yes people" who treat him like a god, Nebuchadnezzar convinces himself that he is one. And this hubris leads to his most harrowing nightmare coming true. He's driven away from the people, akin to Adam and Eve being expelled from the garden, reduced to a Gollum-like creature trotting on all fours. He roams the fields with wild oxen until his hair becomes a tangled mess and his nails yellow and dull, like old bird claws. Whenever he nears the palace, the people avoid eye contact and hush their whisperings about what has happened to their once-great king.

At the appointed time, the human-turned-wild-beast comes to his senses and praises and honors the true King of kings, the Lord of lords, the One who lives forever. Nebuchadnezzar soon hears his vertebrae snap and pop, and for the first time in as long as he can remember, he stands upright, then walks upright, and, most importantly, can now live upright before God.

With his mind and body fully restored, it's time for a long-overdue shower, haircut, and mani-pedi. King Nebuchadnezzar returns to the throne a different man, transformed by the Spirit of God who doesn't waste anything. Even a bout of severe mental illness and a foray into the wild kingdom become the ore the Spirit refines into humility and genuine worship in the heart of a pagan king. It stands as one of the Bible's most remarkable stories of repentance—a murderous dictator coming to know the one true God.

Sometimes we can believe that what we possess is too ordinary for the Spirit to use. That our knowledge or interests are so commonplace, they can't possibly amount to anything significant. That the framed accolades or certificates we've earned are nothing more than dust collectors or ego boosters. That our observations and hard-won life lessons are just basic life hacks. I don't know the subjects you've studied or the stories you've lived. I don't know the geography you've traversed or the people you've met along the way. I don't know the skills you've honed since childhood or those you've cultivated in adulthood. But this much I know: The Spirit doesn't waste anything.

> The Spirit leverages what we consider ordinary to do the extraordinary.

Daniel and his friends remind us that the Spirit leverages what we consider ordinary—our know-how, experience, and circumstances—and puts it to extraordinary use. The Spirit rummages through the pantry of our lives, pulls out everything we've lived and learned, and mixes it all into a delectable divine dish that nourishes the world. Because the Spirit of the one true God does not waste anything.

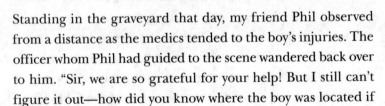

Standing in the graveyard that day, my friend Phil observed from a distance as the medics tended to the boy's injuries. The officer whom Phil had guided to the scene wandered back over to him. "Sir, we are so grateful for your help! But I still can't figure it out—how did you know where the boy was located if you've never visited this cemetery before?"

Phil explained that during his undergraduate years at the University of Alabama, his fascination with American history led him to discover that one of the best ways to study a community's past is through its cemeteries. Burial practices often reveal important clues about the population's values, religious beliefs, economic status, and more. Phil's senior thesis had focused on the Albany Rural Cemetery in New York, and he had meticulously mapped its grounds despite never having set foot there.

For a moment, both men marveled at what less spiritual people might call a "coincidence." Forty years after completing his thesis, Phil found himself in the cemetery the exact day and at the precise time first responders needed directions to rescue a boy.

"I don't know if you ever thought your undergraduate project had real-world value," the officer said, "but today it may have helped save that boy's life."

A coincidence? Perhaps. Or maybe a miracle of the Spirit who wastes nothing.

As Phil ambled out of the cemetery that afternoon, a Scripture he'd read that morning flashed through his mind: "The steps of a man are established by the LORD." He chuckled, recognizing the divine fingerprints on the day's events. Only the Spirit could have orchestrated such details.

As with Daniel and Phil and the scores of believers who've lived and died between them, the Spirit delights in using the details of our lives that we might dismiss or overlook. We can glimpse the Spirit working powerfully this way both in individuals and in entire communities. This is particularly visible when the church gathers people with a diverse range of education, experience, backgrounds, and interests.

I recently heard of a youth group in our town that undertook a weekend river-rafting trip. In the mountains of Utah, the weather can change faster than a blink, and on the second morning of the trip, unexpected storm clouds snuck up on them. The teenagers paddled furiously to outrun the storm, but the driving winds trapped their raft against an island in the middle of the river.

Huddled together, shivering and praying, they were soon joined by another raft swept ashore near them. Despite their own challenges, the youth felt compelled by the Spirit to share their supplies and offer shelter to the strangers.

After the youth prayed again, their leader had an idea. If she could find a high place on the island, she might be able to secure enough cell coverage to send a text to the one person who might be able to help direct them—a retired meteorologist in their congregation. Soon the leader stood on a tall rock, neck and arms craned toward the stormy, windy sky. The message for help went through, and so did the meteorologist's response:

> The storm will last all day, but in three hours, the winds will shift. Move then.

Following the meteorologist's guidance, both rafts navigated safely to the next haul-out area just in time. The expert advice not only saved the youth but also brought relief to the other stranded party.

The *ruach* often plays the long game with our knowledge, interests, gifts, and relationships. The Spirit revives the dormant knowledge of a tourist to rescue a boy trapped under a tombstone. The Spirit unites an adventurous youth group and a retired meteorologist in the same church family, knowing they'll need each other someday. The *ruach* uses the knowledge and giftings of Daniel and Co. to play a crucial role in transforming a king and establishes them as godly leaders in one of the most powerful empires the world has ever seen. And the Spirit will use all *you* possess for the good of others and for God's glory—if you allow it.

At the center of the Christian faith is the belief in an incarnate God who shows up in an unexpected place, at an unexpected time, among unsuspecting people to perform the ultimate rescue. So, we should not be surprised when the Spirit uses the unexpected in our lives—our unique family backgrounds, the places we've lived, and what we've learned through assorted studies, diverse jobs, and niche hobbies. What may seem like a waste, a mistake, or a quirk can become fertile ground for a great work of the Spirit.

> The Spirit will use all you possess for the good of others and for God's glory—if you allow it.

Today, enlarge your vision of the Spirit's work in your life. Trust that the Spirit has placed you within a community where even what appears to be insignificant is being redeemed. Invite the Spirit to employ what seems to be inconsequential and leverage what looks immaterial to help heal and rescue this world. The Spirit, who doesn't waste anything, is waiting to use your everything to accomplish something beyond your imagination.

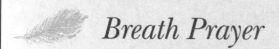

Breath Prayer

BREATHE IN:

Spirit of the Living God

BREATHE OUT:

All I have is yours.

NINE

THE SPIRIT WHO SAYS "GO"

BACK WHEN I WAS IN hot pursuit of the Spirit during college, I heard a rumor about a Methodist conference in Denver that centered around knowing and understanding the Holy Spirit. Jack, my sixtysomething youth pastor and one of the best representations of Jesus I've ever known, kept nudging me to attend.

Because of Jack's persistence, I registered and found myself immersed in lectures that highlighted the Holy Spirit's vibrancy throughout the Bible and in our world today.

One workshop divided us into groups to pray for one another, but instead of sharing personal needs before our prayer time, we were challenged to ask the Holy Spirit how to pray for the others and then trust the Spirit would bring words to mind.

I turned toward the elderly couple next to me. The husband sat in a motorized wheelchair, and it seemed obvious to pray for physical healing. But when I asked the Spirit how to pray, it was as if the *ruach* swept my mind, leaving nothing but a single crumb to think about: the man's relationship with his daughter. This man was a total stranger. I didn't know if he even had a daughter, but what did I have to lose?

Placing my hand on his shoulder, I closed my eyes and prayed aloud for healing in his relationship with his daughter. When I looked up, tears streamed down his cheeks.

"Everyone usually prays for my physical healing," he said, looking up at me with a particular sweetness. "But this is what I need most. The distance between my daughter and me has been breaking my heart."

We both sat there, stunned. That's when I discovered that the Spirit can equip us to pray with precision. To this day, when I pray for someone, I ask, "Lord, how should I pray?"

The Spirit can equip us to pray with precision.

The Spirit continued to surprise me throughout the conference but really showed off on the final afternoon. Sitting in the main ballroom in the stillness of prayer, I felt a distinct but strange thought: *Go to the conference prayer room and look underneath the tables.*

That's weird, I thought. *God isn't like the Easter Bunny, hiding treasures in hotel conference centers. This is silly.*

Yet the thought persisted: *Go to the conference prayer room and look underneath the tables.*

When I considered not obeying, I felt off-balance, like a tight-rope walker who accidentally looks down. The prompting felt harmless, so I decided to follow the nudge. What could it hurt?

I followed the signs to the designated prayer room. It looked ordinary, with tables along the walls, each draped with a crisp white tablecloth touching the floor. Most of those praying had their eyes closed—*phew!*—as I tiptoed to the closest table and peeked underneath. Nothing. A woman looked up and shot me a concerned look, but I shrugged and flashed a toothy grin.

When she bowed her head again, I moved toward the next table. Nothing. Then a third. Nada. A fourth and fifth. Diddly-squat. I lifted the corner of the final tablecloth. That's when I saw it: a worn leather Bible stuffed with papers. *Whoa!* I thought. *The Holy Spirit led me here, but why?* I noticed a name inscribed on the lower left-hand corner of the cover in faded metallic foil.

Scooping up the Bible, I approached each person in the room asking if it belonged to them or someone they knew. *Nope. Not mine. Never seen it. No idea.* But one woman recognized the name and even had the person's contact information. I stepped outside and called the phone number.

"Hi, I'm Margaret, and I found your Bible at the Aldersgate event."

"Really? That's wonderful news!" the woman said. "Where did you find it?"

"Funny story," I said, "but I felt prompted by the Spirit to look under the tables in the prayer room, and there it was."

"You won't believe this," she exclaimed. "I've been praying someone would find it. That Bible is so precious to me and contains decades of notes and photos that mean more than you could possibly know."

The woman lived an hour or so north of Denver, in Loveland, Colorado, and I promised to return the treasure to her that same day. Wonderstruck by the turn of events, I shared the story with a few other conference attendees. One of them, a ministry worker, had been praying for a ride that day to the same area. I shook my head in wonder and offered to give him a lift. Not only did I find my prayers to encounter the Spirit answered, but I recognized the Spirit moving on behalf of others' prayers too.

This unusual string of prompts from the Spirit—*go* to the prayer room, go look under the tables, *go* recover a Bible, *go* give a ride, *go* experience the Spirit's delight in working among a community of believers—remains a significant marker in my spiritual journey. Like the time I woke up with Joel 2 buzzing through my mind, this was one more undeniable encounter with the Spirit of the Living God.

Many of us have heard stories like this, where people follow an inkling from the Spirit and something inexplicable or even miraculous happens. My friend Sherrill shared one that stuck to my bones. A few years ago, just before Christmas, she and her husband, Harvey, were driving an hour to Bristol, New Hampshire, for a church service. A wintery nor'easter sent a blinding snowstorm, and they felt grateful to be the first car behind a snowplow.

Clutching the steering wheel, Sherrill sensed the Holy Spirit prompting her to turn onto a side road. She hesitated but trusted her many years of following the *ruach*'s lead.

"Where are we going?" Harvey protested as they veered off-course.

Sherrill explained her spiritual prodding, and though Harvey wasn't confident, they both agreed to keep going. The side road eventually spit them back onto the main road. That's when they spotted her: a woman lacking hat, gloves, and snow boots running frantically down the road. The couple whizzed past her but felt a pause in their spirits. They knew that anyone venturing out on foot in this weather was in serious trouble.

"We need to go back!" Harvey exclaimed.

Sherrill made a five-point turn, sped back, and rolled down her window. The woman appeared shaken, and not just from the cold. "Do you need help?" Sherrill yelled into the wind.

Without saying a word, the woman jumped into the back seat of their car. Kathleen's story unfolded in fits and spurts: she was in a bad situation . . . sex worker . . . old trailer . . . multiple men . . . physical violence . . . had to escape . . . grabbed coat . . . ran to stay alive . . . nowhere to go.

"I'm so sorry. How can we help?" Sherrill asked. "Can we take you to the police to report this?"

"Nooooo!" Kathleen screamed. "I'll jump out this door right now."

"Okay, okay," Sherrill said, trying to calm her. "Why don't you

stay with us until you figure out what to do next? We're headed
to a church service where you'll be safe. It's warm there, and
afterward we can take you for dinner and find you somewhere
safe to sleep tonight?"

"I'd like that," Kathleen said.

Sherrill's heart ached for the harried woman in her rearview
mirror. Prompted by the same Spirit of the Living God who
had prodded her to take the detour, Sherrill softly asked, "Has
anyone ever told you that God loves you?"

"My great-grandmother said that a lot, but it's always been
hard for me to believe," Kathleen said. "Life is nothing
but pain."

Taking a deep breath, Sherrill prayed for the Spirit to rest on
her lips, and then she spoke of Jesus, his journey, his sacrifice,
his love, and the gift of salvation.

"I want that," Kathleen said.

They prayed together there in the car, and Kathleen invited
Jesus to take control of her troubled life and transform it into
something beautiful.

Sherrill grinned at Kathleen's reflection in the rearview mirror;
she somehow looked brighter. They pulled into the church's
strip-mall parking lot and walked into the service together.
The congregation embraced Kathleen with kindness and
warmth, without a hint of judgment. Kathleen didn't know a
single word of the worship lyrics, but she watched others sing,
arms lifted toward the ceiling. The sermon "just happened"

to center on the relentless love of God. After the service, the trio headed to a cozy local restaurant to discuss Kathleen's next steps.

"I can't believe that I was running for my life just a few hours ago with frozen fingers and numb toes," Kathleen said. "Now I'm at this warm, lovely restaurant with you two, eating a delicious meal and actually feeling hopeful."

"That's the goodness of God," Sherrill said.

Over the next few months, Sherrill and Harvey helped Kathleen find a safe place to live, and she even landed a job. She started attending their small church and rekindled hopes of reconnecting and reconciling with her son one day.

> Life becomes a divine adventure whenever we respond to the Spirit's promptings.

Recalling the story a few years later, Sherrill explained, "We have seen countless professions of faith in Jesus over the years. Kathleen's story is just one. Life becomes a divine adventure whenever we respond to the Spirit's promptings. I can't wait for the next opportunity!"

The triune God delights in moving among communities of believers through a simple command that creates portals for divine adventure. It's a teensy-weensy verb, just two letters in English: *go*. But watch out, because through it, the Spirit of the Living God often unleashes divine power, presence, and purposes.

Our friend Noah was told to *go* into the ark, and Abram to *go* from his homeland. Aaron was told to *go* see his brother, and Balaam to *go* here and there. God keeps Moses on speed dial, instructing him to *go* back to Pharaoh almost a half dozen times. The Spirit speaks the word *go* to and through people who are filled with the Spirit—those whom the Spirit wears like a garment and upon whose lips the Spirit rests: Deborah, Gideon, David, Nathan, Gad, Elijah, Isaiah, Jeremiah, Ezekiel, Hosea, Amos, and many others.

Yet another beautiful example is Simeon, whom the Spirit prompts to *go*. Long before we meet Simeon, the Holy Spirit whispers in his ear, "You will see the Messiah before you die."

Simeon, whose name means "one who hears," is well known throughout his community for being righteous and devout. But I imagine when he shares the Spirit's announcement with his companions, it doesn't go over as well as he expects. Some dear friends likely believe along with him, while others nod politely, and a few think he has fallen off his rocker.

With each passing year, hope for the coming Messiah wanes. Even Simeon begins to wonder if he misheard. But whenever Simeon gets lost in second-guessing, he circles back to the Scriptures, especially Isaiah, for ballast:

> The LORD will lay bare his holy arm
> in the sight of all the nations,
> and all the ends of the earth will see
> the salvation of our God.

Each syllable renews his trust in the promise that one day God will rescue his people.

By the time we meet Simeon in Luke's Gospel, most of the curly white hair atop his head has migrated to his ears, and arthritis has swollen his fingers and toes. After a rough night's sleep, he rolls out of bed with a few extra groans. That's when Simeon is "moved by the Spirit" to *go* to the temple.

Now this doesn't make a lick of logical sense. It's not a high holy day or even a festival, and the timing couldn't have been worse. Simeon keeps a full calendar. He's set aside hours for study, time for a late-morning nosh with neighbors, and the afternoon for wood carving with his grandkids. But the moments the Spirit tells Simeon—and us—to *go* are rarely convenient.

Yet when Simeon hears the Spirit say, "Go!" he knows better than to resist. He cancels his appointments and makes the long trek. Once in the temple court's plaza, he avoids eye contact with the lineup of merchants attempting to sell him their squawking birds, bleating sheep, and "I Heart Jerusalem" T-shirts.

> The moments the Spirit tells us to *go* are rarely convenient.

The line to enter the inner court shuffles forward. Once he steps inside, the pungent scent of sun-heated feces and soured blood takes his breath away. Simeon coughs, then gags, then raises a cloth above his nose and resolves to breathe through his mouth. Strangers and their stressed-out livestock knock against his stiff body. He cranes his neck to see who might be there, but no one stands out.

Meanwhile, the Holy Spirit has been busy on the other side of town. For Mary and Joseph, this is no ordinary day; this is the appointed day. According to Levitical law, forty days after a newborn boy lets out his first cry, the mother must go to the temple and make a sacrifice for her purification, which happens to coincide with the baby boy's dedication.

Joseph had hoped to purchase the best offering possible for his son, but alas, the couple is so close to broke, I imagine them spending the morning rummaging the couch cushions for spare change. When Joseph and Mary reach the merchants outside the temple courts, they snag the only sacrifice they can afford, a humble offering of birds.

That's when Simeon catches something out of the corner of his eye. *Wait . . . is that a woman . . . with a child in her arms?* he wonders. The Holy Spirit surges through Simeon's veins, and he feels a strong magnetic pull. He sees the child's head resting gently in the crook of the woman's elbow, and glimpses the boy's face. Simeon gasps, breathless.

"It's him! It's him!" he mouths, but no sound escapes his lips.

Mary and Joseph, having completed their offering, are about to exit when an exuberant Jewish man with sparkling brown eyes, long in the tooth—and missing a few—makes a beeline toward them.

Any new mother will tell you, when you're holding a newborn, you become invisible: The child is always the star. Yet something about this old man feels different. He peers directly into Mary's eyes, as if he sees through her, into her future. She hands him her infant without hesitation.

Simeon cradles the impossibly cute baby, recognizing more than a child. He sees the salvation of Israel. The happy wonderment of the Spirit floods his soul. Tapping his feet with glee, he looks to the sky and laughs with unrestrained joy:

> Sovereign Lord, as you have promised,
> you may now dismiss your servant in peace.
> For my eyes have seen your salvation.

He holds the delight of God in his arms, the baby's chunky legs kicking in the air. All this man's deepest longings and desires materialize in this miniature package of humanity. Simeon will forever be a witness that God keeps his promises— promises always worth the wait. Simeon blesses Joseph. Simeon blesses Mary. Then, he speaks Spirit-infused, prophetic, soul-penetrating words to the young mom:

> This child is destined to cause the falling and rising
> of many in Israel, and to be a sign that will be spoken
> against, so that the thoughts of many hearts will be
> revealed. And a sword will pierce your own soul too.

I often wonder how many times Mary, who stored meaningful moments in her heart, returned to those words for encouragement, for strength, for understanding. She no doubt carried these words with her, and at times the words most likely carried her—all because the Spirit said, "Go!" and Simeon *went*.

Almost all of us have sensed the Spirit prompting us to *go*. If you're tempted to put up your hands in protest and say, "Nope, not me . . . never," please pause, my friend. Have you never felt the Spirit nudge you to *go* apologize? *Go* mend a relationship? *Go* send an encouraging note? *Go* give a gift? *Go* bake a casserole? *Go* cover someone's tab? *Go* visit someone in the hospital? *Go* share the love of God? *Go* volunteer after a natural disaster or crisis?

Our faith activates through action. The Spirit says "Go!" to us far more often than we realize. But when we sense the call, it's easy to construct cinderblock walls of self-protection:

- *I don't have the time or margin, plus it's inconvenient.*

- *It won't work, it seems silly, or it won't make a difference.*

- *I'm not good enough, holy enough, pure enough, _____ enough.*

- *I'll probably say the wrong words and ruin everything.*

- *If I go, it will feel awkward, or I'll end up embarrassing myself.*

- *I can't be sure this is really the Spirit anyway.*

The path of least resistance will always be *not* to go, *not* to obey, *not* to respond. Yet the best seconds of your day, your week, your month, and possibly even your year might be waiting for you when you sense the Spirit's nudge to *go* and start putting one foot in front of the other.

As with dreams and words and any inklings from the Spirit, we should sift these prompts through the colander of biblical discernment, including 1 Corinthians 13. If the nudge to *go* aligns with God's character and Word, if it ushers you to greater dependence on God and stirs you to greater love for

God and others, then prayerfully and urgently consider taking action.

Often the Spirit's call to *go* arrives with a sense of immediacy. We must "*go* look under the table" *now*, "*go* take the side road" *now*, or, like Simeon, "*go* to the temple" *now*.

You might be wondering, *What if I go, and nothing happens?* Many of us share the same concern. But consider that the Spirit may be working even if you never see it. Just last week, I was swimming laps when I felt prompted to *go* talk to an elderly gentleman in the next lane. We chatted about the

The Spirit may be working even if you never see it.

weather, his travel plans, and random sports teams I knew little about. The whole exchange felt like a nonversation. We didn't touch on faith or anything deep, and I haven't seen the man since.

Did I misunderstand the Spirit? Perhaps. But I'll never know what the Spirit might have accomplished through that exchange. Perhaps it made my fellow swimmer feel less lonely. Or encouraged him that the pool serves as a great place to connect with others. Or maybe it was an opportunity for me to practice quick obedience. Or perhaps I needed to lay off the late-night moo goo gai pan with all its extra MSG. Even if I was mistaken, showing kindness to a stranger because of it is still a win—and I bet God thinks so too.

Whenever our actions reflect God's character and ways as revealed in Scripture, we don't need to fret over whether there was too much static when we heard the Spirit. The bigger risk is being so afraid of making mistakes that we never *go* at all.

Our heavenly Father takes great pleasure and joy in our fumbling attempts to respond to the Spirit.

Any parent will tell you that when children first learn to speak and respond, there's no telling what they'll say or do. If parents say, "Go to the kitchen and come back with a spoon," the child might wander into the living room or return with a ladle—but the adoring parents' response isn't to scold. They're thrilled their child moved in the general direction and—*gadzooks*—remembered to come back. The parents will embrace the child and celebrate the win. They'll keep giving more opportunities for the child to *go*. And one day, that child will return from the kitchen spoon in hand. What a celebration—not because the child needs to be perfect, but because of the parents' faithfulness. They know this is just the beginning of so much more goodness for their child.

> You're invited to the daily wonders and joy of being part of the Spirit's work in the world.

This process of sending and responding in human parenting comes from the Parent of all parents, our triune God. The way we teach our children, when we do it well, mirrors the way God teaches his beloved children to respond. The Spirit keeps offering opportunities to *go*. Opportunities to become more and more attuned to God's desires and the way the Spirit works in the world. Opportunities to enter the daily wonders and joy of being part of the Spirit's work in the world. It's a privilege and delight that the Creator of All wants to be with us, to work in us and through us in accomplishing his purposes. Endless divine adventures await when we answer the prompt to *go*.

My dear friend Will says one of the best decisions he made in his late twenties was creating a "personal board" to guide his life. Much like a corporate board of directors, the members hailed from diverse backgrounds, each offering unique skills and perspectives. Over the last forty years, these individuals have become some of the most influential voices in Will's life, with many becoming close personal friends.

One of Will's board members, Bob, once challenged him: "You're smart, articulate, and successful, but you struggle to share the good news of Jesus one-on-one with strangers. I know it can feel awkward, but you need to do it. And you need to do it in a place where you'll be totally dependent on the Spirit."

"Where do you suggest I go?" Will asked.

"Cuba," Bob replied. "You don't speak or understand Spanish, which is perfect. And I know a nonprofit that can get you there."

A few months later, Will and a half dozen other believers stepped off a plane in Havana for a six-day visit. They crammed into a creaky van and puttered along to a poverty-stricken neighborhood on the outskirts of town. A grid of mostly one-story cinderblock houses lined the streets. The van pulled over, and the travelers climbed out. After a brief prayer, they each headed in different directions, accompanied by their translators.

Will looked up and down the street, spotted a two-story structure, and decided, *I'll start there.*

As he climbed the somewhat decrepit cement stairs, Will

rehearsed how he'd introduce himself to strangers. *Hi, I'm Will, and I'm from America. We're just ninety miles away. I'm in Cuba to find out what Cubans think about God.*

Standing before a weathered ivory door with peeling paint, Will drew in a breath and tapped his knuckles on the door. A pair of dogs started barking. A man cracked open the door and peered out. Will froze for a split second, then recited his spiel like a vacuum salesman: "Hi, I'm Will, and I'm from America . . . What do Cubans think about God?"

The man threw up his hand. "*Bastante!*" he said (meaning "Enough!"). "*Tienes un mensaje de Dios. Cuéntame que es eso!*"

"You have a message for me from God," the interpreter translated. "Tell me what it is!"

Will's jaw gaped open. Before he could utter a word, the man, whose name was Carlos, started spewing words in Spanish, his hands flying in all directions. He appeared bouncy and alert, though without a hint of agitation.

The interpreter pieced together his story. Like many Cubans, Carlos worked two jobs to survive. His "official" job, sponsored by the state government, paid almost nothing. His second "unofficial" job involved buying blank cassette tapes, making recordings, and reselling them. The latter had fed his family for decades.

Several months before Will's visit, someone broke into Carlos's home and stole his duplicator. He lost his livelihood. Carlos knew the police would do nothing, so he spread the word among his friends and neighbors and prayed for the machine's return. Weeks passed, then months. Carlos blamed God for putting him in a position where he struggled to support his family.

"If you ever want me to trust in you," Carlos fumed at God, "then you must return my duplicator!"

The day before Will's arrival, someone knocked on Carlos's door. It was his son, Miguel. They'd been estranged for many years, so Carlos was baffled to see him.

"Dad, I know where your tape duplication machine is," Miguel said, offering an explanation for his sudden appearance.

"How did you even know it was missing?" Carlos asked. "You haven't been here in years."

Miguel explained that he'd been partying with some friends when he saw a duplicator in the room that he'd never seen there before. Taking a closer look, he recognized a sticker he'd placed on the machine as a boy. That's when he knew it was his dad's.

"I know you'd never let it go," Miguel said. "It's your livelihood. Let's go get it back."

Carlos hugged his son. "I've missed you, Miguelito."

"Me too, Papa."

Miguel led Carlos to the house where he'd seen the machine. Sure enough, it was still there. No one was home, so Carlos took back what was rightfully his.

Carlos led Will and the translator into his living room, proudly pointing to the duplicator.

"Now you are here, an American in Cuba, standing at my door talking about God," Carlos said, waving his arms like water from a broken sprinkler head. "Whatever message you have for me, I know it must be from God, because only he can do things like this. So tell it to me now because that's why you're here in Cuba."

"Uh, I wanted to tell you about my friend Jesus," Will stammered. He shared pieces of his own life story and the personal transformation he had experienced because of a loving God.

"I want Jesus," Carlos said. Right there and then, he prayed to receive Christ's forgiveness and rescue.

Before they even said "Amen," neighbors from around the block had gathered at the top of the stairs and peeked through the door. *What was an American doing in their neighborhood?* Word of mouth travels fast in Cuba's streets.

Carlos waved them inside and started to explain all that had just transpired.

"I was ill-prepared for what I was experiencing," Will recalls. "I was honestly just treading water, trying to stay in the moment."

The visitors started asking questions about Jesus. Following Will's responses, more people believed. Before he could finish praying with them, more people filled the living room. Will repeated his stories of being transformed by God's infinite love and even more people believed in Jesus.

This continued for hours. When the time came for Will to leave, over forty people had packed into Carlos's house, some crammed in the stairwell, some even hanging out of window frames—all to hear about Jesus.

"That was just the first door we knocked on," Will recalls. "There were so many more—and what I didn't know at the time was that my other six friends were having similar experiences."

Will remembers one rickety staircase he climbed in a different area of the city. A woman greeted him and the translator at the door and welcomed them inside, where a few older women were gathered. Most homes he'd visited had a couple of chairs and a makeshift sofa, but this one was well appointed with hefty wooden furniture, glass windows, and a huge Cuban flag hanging in the center of the living room.

"Did you come to pray for Antonio?" the woman asked through the translator.

By this point, Will was so expectant for the Holy Spirit's leading that he enthusiastically nodded "*Sí!*" though he had no idea what to expect.

The woman led him to a large bedroom toward the back of the house where a man lay in bed, a nurse hovering nearby. Antonio's eyes were closed; he was seemingly napping, unbothered by Will.

"I just prayed a simple prayer," Will recalls. "I prayed for Antonio's health, for the health of the home, and for the country of Cuba. I prayed for people to come to know Jesus."

As Will prayed, Antonio opened his eyes and looked up. The woman who had welcomed Will into the house shrieked. The other women rushed in and screamed, hugging Antonio, who hugged them back. Everyone was yelling in Spanish, the whole commotion confusing Will.

With all the ruckus, Will decided to slip out with the translator and regroup on the street. "What just happened?" Will asked the interpreter. "What did we do wrong?"

"Oh, you don't understand," the translator explained. "Antonio has been in a coma for years, and he's just woken up."

We are called to live in step with the Spirit. Before Jesus departed, he gave one of the most famous "go" statements of all time:

> Therefore *go* and make disciples of all nations,
> baptizing them in the name of the Father and of the
> Son and of the Holy Spirit, and teaching them to
> obey everything I have commanded you. And surely
> I am with you always, to the very end of the age.

Many of us want to obey Jesus's command, but the magnitude of it feels overwhelming. I believe the *go* the Spirit leads us toward begins in our own neighborhoods and communities—not just someday but every day. It might involve a plane ticket to somewhere far away like it did for Will, but more often, it happens where we find ourselves today.

When the Spirit says "Go!" and you obey, who knows what might happen? What role might you play in the answer to someone's prayer? What help might you give to someone God is rescuing from a bad situation? What person might you meet who comes to faith? What miracle might you see? What healing might you be part of? All those little prompts and nudges to *go* matter more than you realize. And through them, the Spirit works mightily.

Let's listen for the Spirit's call, and let's *go*!

 Breath Prayer

BREATHE IN:

Spirit of the Living God

BREATHE OUT:

Wherever you lead, I'll go.

TEN

THE SPIRIT WHO HEALS DIVIDES

PERHAPS YOU'VE NOTICED THAT DIVISIONS among people seem more pronounced and pervasive than ever before, widening the once-narrow gaps of differences into seemingly insurmountable chasms in our relationships. Sometimes the ensuing divides in friendships and families can seem intractable. But bridging these chasms is one of the Holy Spirit's specialties—as I've seen firsthand.

More than a decade before my Jewish father became a follower of Jesus while hiding in a camouflage turkey blind, he noticed surfing was growing in popularity along the shores of South Florida. On a whim, my dad borrowed a friend's fiberglass board, paddled out, and caught his first wave. He was hooked.

Despite an abundance of naysayers who assessed the sport as

nothing more than a passing fad, my dad was convinced it was here to stay. He enlisted a few fellow surfers, who were also gifted artists, to make a series of boards. Single and unattached, he began driving up the East Coast from South Florida to Maine, introducing his brand, Oceanside Surfboards, to coastal stores. Years of making the long trek paid off: My dad became the largest manufacturer of surfboards on the East Coast.

Along the way, Dad crossed paths with Jack Murphy, also known as "Murf the Surf," fresh off winning a statewide surfing competition in Florida. My father befriended the tall, charming beach icon, unaware of the unsavory path Jack was already headed down—and the impact that it would eventually have on him.

When Jack wasn't riding waves, he was swindling guests at Miami Beach's famed Casablanca Hotel, partnering with a hotel employee who was also a con artist. The scheme started with pilfering jewelry from Casablanca's clientele. But alas, there's only so much you can steal from a single hotel before you get caught, so they moved on, expanding their grift to the mansions that dotted the Intracoastal Waterway. Their getaway method was as ingenious as their heists: Jack would leap into the water and swim away with the booty to evade capture.

The crimes were easy to rationalize since they appeared victimless. The jewels were insured, the owners were reimbursed, and no one got hurt. Plus, the daring adventures funded the party boys' boozy, Cadillac-and-yacht lifestyle. When the smaller thefts lost their thrill, Jack decided to up the ante, plotting a weekend of heists in New York with friends, including targeting a Hamptons socialite. But after a wild night in the city, they set their sights higher: the jewel collection at the American Museum of Natural History.

Surveying the museum, they couldn't believe their luck. The alarm on the display case for the famed Star of India—a 563.35-carat sapphire—was corroded. Even better, the museum left twenty windows open day and night for ventilation, and budget cuts meant a lone security guard with only a flashlight for protection sporadically checked the collection.

On October 29, 1964, Murf the Surf and his cohorts scaled the walls of the American Museum of Natural History, outmaneuvered the lone security guard, and absconded with two dozen priceless jewels, including the Star of India, the DeLong Star Ruby, and the sixteen-carat Eagle Diamond. The audacious caper would become known as the "Jewel Heist of the Century."

Just two days later, the men were apprehended. While awaiting trial for the museum robbery, Jack and one of his associates faced separate charges for robbing and assaulting actress Eva Gabor. (Yep, that's right. You can't make this stuff up.) Jack negotiated a lighter sentence by offering to reveal the location of the jewels, some of which were retrieved from a Miami bus station locker, but the Eagle Diamond was never found.

Jack was released from prison a few years later. That's when his life took an even darker turn. He delved into embezzlement and assault and even committed first-degree murder. The once-beloved, charming surf icon found himself imprisoned for two life sentences with hard labor.

Before that final sentencing, the police and FBI sometimes

turned to my father to ask about Jack's whereabouts. Law enforcement assumed my dad's ties to the surfing community might yield insights, but my father had lost all contact with Jack long ago. The authorities kept asking anyway.

A strange turn of events befell my father during those years: One morning he received devastating news from the fire department that his surfboard manufacturing business had burned to the ground. While the fire was officially labeled as "undetermined in origin," the fire chief privately suspected foul play and believed that someone had started the blaze intentionally.

When my father went to file the insurance claim, he realized he had stored the sole paper copy of his insurance policy in his office, which had gone up in flames. Without proof of coverage, the insurance company rejected his claim.

Undeterred, my father plunged into debt to rebuild his company. Just months after the grand reopening, the fire chief called again: My father's manufacturing facility had burned to the ground a second time. Though the cause remained officially undetermined once again, suspicions of arson and the most likely arsonist lingered. Law enforcement later confirmed that Jack thought my dad was collaborating with the police to capture him. They knew Jack was responsible for the fires but lacked evidence to convict him.

Unable to secure insurance after the first fire, my father lost everything once more.

The cumulative losses were crushing. Newly married, my parents now had to claw their way out of what felt like a bottomless pit of debt. When adjusted for inflation, creditors were calling to the tune of almost $1,000,000.00.

Gathered around the supper table with my parents as a child, I grew up listening to stories of their struggles during this period—double shifts seven days a week, surviving on a fifty-pound bag of brown rice gifted by a friend, navigating impatient debt collectors, and the long years it took to pay back every last cent. The agony and distress Jack Murphy left in his wake were immeasurable. My father hoped he'd never have to lay eyes on Jack again.

While the debt eventually disappeared, the scars of anguish remained. Even over half a century later, I still catch the pained expression on my mom's face when their bank account dips too low. My parents know what it's like to have their life sabotaged by someone else's actions, and I've watched them work tirelessly to ensure they never face such devastation again.

Even if no one has ever literally burned your livelihood to the ground, my hunch is that somewhere along the way you've felt the sting of someone else's thoughtless behavior, selfish decisions, or ruthless exploits.

Some of these people rank among the lighter fare: perhaps a person you dodge at the grocery store, deflect by sending to voicemail, or "accidentally" block on social media. Others, like Jack Murphy, you hope to never see again. Maybe their actions caused the grievous loss of something—or worse, someone—you loved. Out of this hurt, you wake up one day and discover a great divide in your relationship, and restoration, let alone healing, feels impossible.

Yet these are the very spaces where the Holy Spirit performs some of the most delightful work.

Sometimes I wonder what the disciples first thought upon awakening the morning after the crucifixion, realizing the rabbi with whom they had invested the last three years of their lives was gone. I imagine some felt like they'd been conned; others, like everything they'd worked for had burned to the ground.

Just days prior, when the disciples had gathered around the table with Jesus to celebrate Passover, something probably felt "off." They carried that uneasy feeling that comes when you know something terrible is going to happen, and while you don't know what it is, you know you can't stop it. They didn't know they'd soon watch Jesus tread an unexpected road: a public arrest, an unfair trial, a criminal's execution, and a heart-wrenching cry: "My God, my God, why have you forsaken me?"

Jesus too was keenly aware that this season of ministry together with his beloved followers—and even his very life—was coming to an end. He wanted to bestow a parting gift, something they'd treasure forever.

What do you give to someone you love so much that you're willing to die for them?

Many years ago, I cared for a family whose children I cherished deeply. On the eve of my departure, their devoted mother, Monica, gifted me a precious box containing a hand-carved, exquisitely detailed mirror. This mirror has accompanied me through countless moves, and each time I glimpse it, I feel the warmth of that family's love.

The gift someone gives you before they or you depart is often the most meaningful. Whether it's the tender words whispered before a last breath, the note someone slips into your hand before they move away, or the package placed in your palm before a farewell—the gift can remain with you forever.

Jesus could have flooded the Sea of Galilee with fish or handed the disciples suitcases of gold. But Jesus was no talk-show host exclaiming, "You get a chariot, you get a chariot, you get a chariot!" Instead, Jesus handpicked the most meaningful gift of all:

> And I will ask the Father, and he will give you
> another *advocate* to help you and be with you forever.

The Greek word translated as "advocate," *parakletos*, encompasses roles like helper, counselor, comforter, and strengthener— beautiful attributes of the Spirit of the Living God. The One who carries us, leads us, guides us, and reminds Christ's disciples—both then and now—of all Jesus said. The One who lifts our burdens and carries them for us. The One who never abandons us and always remains with us. These are just some of the ways the Spirit has been loving humans since the dawn of time.

This is the same Spirit who hovered over the *tohu wa vohu*, inspired Joseph's dreams, and empowered Bezalel, Oholiab, and the artisans. This is the same *ruach* who spoke through David, wore Gideon, and breathed hope into Ezekiel and the exiles, who enhanced the abilities of Daniel and wooed Simeon to the temple with the instruction to "go." This Spirit of the Living God overshadowed Mary, prophesied through Elizabeth, filled John the Baptist before birth, and descended like a dove at Jesus's baptism. This is the same Spirit who led Jesus into the desert, empowered the seventy to perform mighty miracles, and helped raise Jesus from the dead.

Tucked away with his followers, Jesus promises to bestow the most magnificent, delightful gift. Rather than gifting us *something*, Jesus gives us *Someone*.

We've learned much about this promised *Someone* as we've walked the road toward Pentecost together. Our journey has spanned over three thousand years, and our understanding of the Spirit of the Living God has expanded with every footfall. So, nothing that happens next should surprise us.

Now, in an upper room after Jesus's death and ascension, the disciples and a hundred or so others are stacked like tinned sardines. They've been storm-tossed by recent events, discombobulated by the swirl of confusion and heartbreaking loss. Yet the Spirit meets them in their mayhem. Each person there carries with them a different piece of the glorious puzzle of Jesus's time on earth. Some gather around tables while others sit on rugs or pillows or benches. The artisans who crafted that building, that room, that furniture likely had no idea that what they made would make such a difference for those gathered.

Over the past fifty days, the Spirit of the Living God has been working in the waiting—giving Jesus's beloved followers time to process, to remember, to sort through what they've seen, experienced, and learned. And of course, nothing is wasted. Luke underscores their unity, "*all together* in *one* place," setting the stage for what is to come.

Without warning, the sound of a squall-like wind fills the building—the holy *ruach*. Light travels faster than sound, but in this crowded room, they hear the Spirit before they see the Spirit's handiwork: tongues of fire hovering over each person. In the Torah and among the prophets, fire often symbolized a purifying agent as well as the presence of God, like the billowing flames that led God's people through the wilderness and the coal that cleansed Isaiah's lips.

The Holy Spirit fills each person and, one might say, wears them like a garment. Tongues of fire spark unfamiliar languages in the believers as the Spirit speaks through them. A crowd soon gathers of God-fearing Jews who had walked up to a thousand miles or so from as far as Mesopotamia, Egypt, Libya, and Rome to celebrate the festival. The syllables sound like gibberish to those who utter them, but for those within earshot, every word bears a divine gift. The Galileans are declaring the mighty wonders of God in dozens of languages they've never spoken before.

Some onlookers observe, mouths agape at the Spirit's presence; others roll their eyes, dismissing the ragamuffins as those who imbibed too much wine. But this isn't a group of boozy babblers. Peter, the restored one, rises to the occasion and traces the work of the Holy Spirit through the words of David, the prophetic promises of Joel, and the miracles of Christ.

The Spirit's spark becomes an unstoppable blaze. Not long after Peter's sermon, Stephen rises and delivers a Spirit-infused speech declaring the star-studded work of God through Christ, but the message falls on rocky hearts and the hearers stone him to death. Persecution erupts throughout Jerusalem and believers run for their lives, with the good news of Jesus and the power of the Holy Spirit accompanying them wherever they go.

At first, it looks like Philip has drawn the short straw. He stashes himself away in Samaria, the epicenter of a people group detested by Jews for more than five hundred years. Samaritans differed in their theology, approach to marriage, and political views, so some Jewish people at the time considered them vermin.

Philip carries a singular message: Jesus. Instead of shrinking back from the Jewish preacher, crowds gather. Instead of interrupting, crowds listen intently. Instead of judging, crowds receive the good news eagerly. The Samaritans watch in awe as those who were paralyzed spin cartwheels and evil spirits vanish in a flash.

It's not just the *Samaritans* who experience the Holy Spirit's power healing divisions. Philip soon encounters Simon, a sorcerer and medium, one of "those kinds of people" deemed off-limits to devout Jews. Yet Simon desires to follow Jesus. Before Philip can wrap his theological head around what's happening, Simon is baptized and follows Philip like a (formerly) lost puppy.

It's not just *Samaritans* and *sorcerers* who experience the Spirit bridging divides. The Holy Spirit directs Philip to stand by an Ethiopian eunuch's chariot. Not only is the eunuch a foreigner, but worse, he is a slave or servant whose genitals have been crushed or cut off. Castrated males were abhorred by some in ancient Jewish communities and were long refused participation in communal life. As a result, long-held prejudices, intolerance, and judgments swirled among some people. Yet at the Holy Spirit's prompting, Philip rushes over and finds the eunuch reading Isaiah. Philip then shares the good news of Jesus, leading to the eunuch's baptism.

The *Samaritans* and *sorcerers* and *eunuchs* are just the beginning. Acts continues to showcase the Holy Spirit healing a divided world through even more unexpected encounters:

- Ananias is tasked with approaching Saul, the man who held the cloaks of those who stoned Stephen. Ananias places his hands on the hate-filled religious terrorist, and Saul is filled with the Holy Spirit and sees more clearly than he ever has before.

- Barnabas cashes in his influencer chips and validates Saul's conversion story to the suspicious disciples. Despite their doubts and fears, they welcome Saul to proclaim Jesus alongside them.

- The Roman commander Cornelius, a leader in the military oppressing the Jewish people, accepts Jesus too. When Peter makes a divine house call, the Holy Spirit floods everyone's hearts, including the uncircumcised gentile friends and relatives within earshot. The oneness initiated here marks the rich beginnings of Jewish-gentile table fellowship.

One of the trademarks of the Spirit is building bridges, not barriers, and this restorative work of the Spirit is anchored in the character of God. The Spirit creates opportunities to reenter relationship. And the healing, grace, and forgiveness that pour forth from the Spirit's work don't just restore minds and emotions and bodies—they restore people to their rightful place in human society.

I was raised to believe that Acts was a book full of sparkly miracles, and indeed it is. But take another look, and you'll see something deeper: the Holy Spirit healing a divided world, transforming our understanding of who is welcome in God's family. (Spoiler alert: Everyone!)

> The Holy Spirit transforms our understanding of who is welcome in God's family.

Acts serves as a sequel to the Gospel of Luke, in which Jesus relentlessly pursues those on the fringes—those marginalized by others, plagued by poor choices, or born with an impairment. It doesn't matter if you're hungry, have traded your integrity for wealth, or are living recklessly, Luke's message is clear: Jesus has come to redeem every last person, from the center of society to the farthest margin, though it has cost him everything.

This drumbeat continues in Luke's second volume, Acts, where the Holy Spirit uses everything from heavenly visions to death-defying miracles to extend a wider welcome to God's table. And at Pentecost, the Spirit uses foreign tongues to unite people who otherwise couldn't communicate and visions to bring together those who would never mingle.

With every new friendship, with every bias upended, with every prejudice proved wrong, God's kingdom expands exponentially, bringing the good news of forgiveness in Christ and healing to a fractured world.

Something changed for Jack Murphy as he served two life sentences in the slammer. Champions for Life, a prison ministry once led by Cleveland Browns star Bill Glass, visited the penitentiary to share the gospel through a troupe of NFL stars. As Jack listened, he pondered the possibility of faith, and something stirred within him. That ember of curiosity soon burst into a flaming faith.

Once a hardened criminal who started one of the biggest riots in the history of Florida State Prison, Jack transformed into a model prisoner. He even began working alongside the prison chaplain. After nearly two decades behind bars, Jack was given early release with lifetime parole. His response? Joining Champions for Life to minister to inmates like himself, traveling and spreading hope where there once was only despair.

My dad, skeptical of another one of Jack's cons, had heard about Jack's work and needed to see for himself. He traveled to attend one of Jack's prison presentations, quietly observing from the back as Murf the Surf mesmerized the audience with tales of daring criminal escapades and the impact of faith on his life.

Was the transformation genuine? my dad wondered. My father remained cautious, opting to keep distant tabs on Jack and his ministry. Stories circulated about Jack's flourishing work among the incarcerated, how he had blossomed into a passionate evangelist. Over time, my dad's heart softened toward Jack, and forgiveness slowly began to take root.

Nearly two decades later, my dad's phone rang. "Hello?"

"Bill, it's Jack Murphy. I'm here in Steamboat with my son and some ministry sponsors," he said. "We're here skiing."

"This is unexpected," my dad replied. "It's been years."

"I know," Jack said earnestly. "You've been on my mind a lot, and I wanted to reach out. Could you join us skiing?"

"Skiing, huh?" my dad said, with a hint of amusement.

"Yeah, the weather's perfect, and I heard the snow is fantastic," Jack said. "I just want a chance to show you that I value our friendship and that I've learned from my mistakes."

"Alright, let's go skiing then. But remember, I'll be keeping my eye on you," my dad replied playfully.

So my father spent the day skiing with the notorious jewel thief, cat burglar, and convicted murderer who had twice sabotaged his life by burning down his business. As they rode the ski lifts together, the conversation flowed effortlessly, though my father sensed there was something Jack wanted to say but struggled to articulate.

Toward the end of the afternoon, my dad invited Jack over for dinner. "Can I bring my son and his friend?" Jack asked.

"Of course."

Around the table, silver-haired Jack, his million-watt smile and goatee gleaming, shared stories of the miraculous transformations he had witnessed among prisoners. Late into the night, my parents and Jack exchanged tales of faith, their hearts stirred as they recounted the Holy Spirit's workings in each of their lives.

As they spoke, Jack's son's friend leaned in. "I want what you have," he declared.

"Would you like to become a follower of Jesus?" my dad gently inquired.

"Yes, I would," he affirmed.

That night, the Holy Spirit orchestrated the impossible. People who never imagined being together in the same room again mingled like old friends. Those who had every reason to harbor suspicion or bias extended olive branches of trust. The Spirit drew them together around God's ever-welcoming table, and as they gathered, the Lord "added to their number" those who were being saved.

After that visit, my dad and Jack didn't maintain close contact. Yet my dad had a lingering sense that Jack still had something on his heart he couldn't quite express. Years later, a mutual lifelong surfing buddy, Bill Yerkes, revealed that Jack had traveled to Steamboat Springs back then with the intention of apologizing to my father for the arsons he had committed but had never found the courage to do so.

The Spirit works to heal divides.

Despite the unspoken words, during their brief time together, the Spirit worked to mend their divide. When my father was inducted into the East Coast Surfing Hall of Fame a few years

later, Jack Murphy stood proudly in the audience, paying trib-
ute to him.

My hunch is that you, like me, have at least one fractured
relationship in your life. Perhaps it's with the neighbor who
displays yard signs or social media posts that tout a different
political party, or a coworker whose decisions clash with yours.
It could be a family member who ignores your calls, the parent
you dread interacting with, a spouse who seems emotionally
distant, or a child whose lifestyle choices you don't approve. Or
maybe it's someone who betrayed your trust, embezzled from
you, or sabotaged your life.

What if the Spirit is orchestrating restoration for that relationship? What if, behind the scenes, the Spirit is crafting a new
beginning? What if the Spirit is planting seeds that will blos-
som into mutual understanding and deep compassion?

Maybe the journey to reconciliation begins in a counselor's
office, as you take the first steps toward healing and forgiveness. Perhaps it's sparked by a phone call, an apology, or a
series of heartfelt letters. It might involve honest reflection on
biases and prejudices that were inherited from family members but that it's time to offload. Or there may come a day
when the Spirit whispers, *Now, go!* and you try once again, and
there's a reunion of hearts, a healing of wounds.

The Holy Spirit's healing isn't limited to one person or one
relationship at a time. The *ruach* can move simultaneously in
the hearts of many—dozens, hundreds, even entire nations.
Two people who couldn't see the world more differently can

enter the same room and, through a moment of prayer or genuine connection, experience shifts in their perspectives or agendas or outcomes that they never thought possible.

As you experience the Holy Spirit healing the divisions in your personal world, you'll find the Spirit nudging you to bring healing to the divides of our larger world. Be ready. Be willing. And rest assured: The Spirit will be by your side every step of the way. After all, the Spirit has been here since the beginning, since the curtain rose on the dawn of time.

"In the beginning, God . . ."

That's where we first discover the God who speaks, the Jesus who creates, and the Spirit who hovers over our *tohu wa vohu* and moves in our mayhem. The One who works the night shift and speaks through our dreams. The Spirit who uses what we make to make a difference and who wears us like a garment. The One who purifies our speech and who rests on our tongues. The Spirit who sometimes works in stages, and who wastes nothing, even as we wait. The One who says "Go!" and remains by our side, bringing healing to our divided world.

Truly, this is the God we need to embrace and understand. This is the God we need to know.

With all my love,

♡ Margaret ♡

Breath Prayer

BREATHE IN:

Spirit of the Living God

BREATHE OUT:

Use me to bring healing to this divided world.

FUN PHOTOS

My mom and dad, Marjane and Bill, in the late 1960s on Christmas morning. *Chapter 1.*

Courtesy of the Feinbergs

Courtesy of the Feinbergs

My mom and dad in the early 1970s after they had come to know Jesus, seen here with their two dogs, Diablo and Becket. *Chapter 1.*

Leif Oines

Early in our marriage, Leif and I lived in Juneau, Alaska. We loved to go to the Mendenhall Glacier. Leif and I would walk on the frozen lake at its base during the winters. *Chapter 3.*

While we lived in Juneau, Leif and I were constantly in awe of the stunning outdoors. This is the Mendenhall River during a spring snow melt near the capital city. *Chapter 3.*

Courtesy of Margaret Feinberg

Some of the bottles Susie brought me were teensy-weensy, but they breathed hope and courage into me. I'll never forget the deep meaning of all the "pieces." *Chapter 4.*

Margaret Feinberg

Preparing to deliver joy through flowers because of Susie's obedience to the Spirit. Indeed, the Holy Spirit didn't waste any of the "pieces." *Chapter 4.*

Margaret Feinberg

Students and visitors on the Asbury campus praying during the outpouring. *Chapter 5.*

Photo courtesy of Asbury University

I KNOW that THERE IS NO ONE That LOVES YOUR LIFE, HEART, MIND, SOUL, MORE THAN THAN THE ONE WHO FORMED IT. YOU HAVE ALWAYS BEEN THE ONE I'VE FOUGHT FOR. LET GO OF THE SWORD YOU HOLD, AND REST... I AM SO PROUD OF YOU...

Margaret Feinberg

The note pressed into my palm by the painter at the conference. The Spirit used the artist's words to deliver a message I desperately needed: It was time to put down my sword. *Chapter 6.*

This is the cottage my parents built on Tillou Cay in the Bahamas as the Spirit worked in the waiting. *Chapter 7.*

Marjane Feinberg

My father and I fighting back with joy on the last day of his cancer treatment. *Chapter 7.*

Leif Oines

My mom and dad will continue to live on a boat and sail through the Bahamas as long as the Spirit gives them breath. *Chapter 7.*

Margaret Feinberg

ABUNDANT GRATITUDE

I WROTE THIS BOOK NAKED.

Once I had developed a map for crafting the content, I discovered a peculiar phenomenon: Whenever I sat down to write, red, swollen, itchy dots appeared all over my body. I'd never seen or experienced anything like it before. Seeking relief, I visited a doctor who identified the malady as hives. Now here's what is fascinating: If I tackled any other project or kind of work, I was hive-free. The hives only appeared when I wrote this book on the Holy Spirit. And erupt they did, every single time I sat down to write, over a period of many agonizing months.

I consulted multiple doctors, but their suggestions and prescriptions were either ineffective or made me sleepy. Yes, the Spirit works the night hours, but one needs to be awake to write a manuscript. I discovered that anything that touched the hives increased their itchiness, so that's how I ended up writing this book naked.

In some ways, it represented the vulnerability that I still feel; sharing intimate stories of my life and faith felt daunting yet necessary. And I'm still in the process of learning all these things for myself. I'm far from perfect and stumble daily, so know that I'm on the journey with you.

I leaned on close friends like Janella Martinez as well as my online community through my e-newsletter and asked them to pray. Their petitions sustained me through the miserable itchy episodes. The support of all those friends remains a testament to the power of collective faith, for which I am deeply thankful.

This book would not exist without the guidance, prayer, and love of my dear friend Jonathan Merritt. We've been sounding boards for each other's works for over two decades. He flew out to Utah, and we spent three long days sorting through the chaotic list of Scriptures and stories that I'd compiled.

Jonathan remarked, "In two decades of collaboration, this is the hardest book you've ever tried to write."

"Thank you for affirming that," I said. "I've been feeling it all along."

We kept trying different methods to shape the book, but they didn't work. So we prayed and waited. We watched in awe of what emerged: a book that reflected the presence of the Holy Spirit in different eras of Israel's history.

When we arrived at the final chapter—the hardest one to shape—we read through Acts 2 and our jaws dropped to the ground. All the elements of the Holy Spirit that we'd unpacked in the previous chapters were present at Pentecost. While this may be obvious to others, we were wonderstruck. We bowed to the ground and worshiped. The Spirit had been working through the mayhem and in the waiting all along. If you see Jonathan online, give him a big hug—he deserves it.

I owe immense gratitude to two theological whizzes who have been kind enough to offer feedback for almost twenty years: Tracee Hackel and Craig Blomberg, whose insights refined the content, ensuring its biblical integrity. In writing, the difference between beautiful writing and heresy are usually just an adverb or adjective away—and they saved me on multiple occasions.

Along the way I made a new friend, Jack Levison. He's written many wonderful books on the Holy Spirit, including *40 Days with the Holy Spirit: Fresh Air for Every Day*. I'm a superfan. While I originally agreed to this project, the topic of the Holy Spirit soon felt so enormous that I became paralyzed. Levison's rich academic work on the Holy Spirit helped me focus on the Old Testament and the oft-overlooked power and presence of the Spirit on the road to Pentecost. His feedback, emails, and insights made this book so much better.

As I was writing the chapter entitled "The Artisan Spirit," I felt prompted that like Bezalel and Oholiab, I needed to surround myself with people of skill. I prayed the Spirit would bring the right people. My dear friend Andrea Townsend spent dozens of hours sharpening and bringing clarity to every sentence. She is such a gift to me. I'm grateful for readers including Susie Nelson and daniel Baltzer (yes, lowercase *d*). Writers including Ken Rummer, Happy Thorp, and Laura Johnson offered their encouragement and semicolons. Terri Fullerton, a gifted writer herself, suggested details to add to the stories that proved invaluable. Jennifer Jones, Sarah Baldwin, and Tara Lantieri encouraged me through their edits and feedback. I met up with Jennifer Grant and Jon Mathieu at the Festival of Faith and Writing. They generously contributed corrections and ideas to the manuscript. I laughed with joy as I experienced the very phenomenon I'd written about coming alive—artisans bringing their gifts and making a difference.

I'm thankful for the loving support of Lori and Jud Wilhite—who have been champions of my writing and teaching for years. I'm grateful for all the friends who shared their stories, some of whom also offered firsthand fact-checking, including Bill Townsend, Bill Yerkes, Phil Waldrep, Cindy Topping, Marjane and Bill Feinberg, Sherrill and Harvey Cobley, and more. I'm thankful for Carolyn McCready, who believed in this book when it was just a seedling of an idea.

I'm grateful for the team at Zondervan: Keren Baltzer, Beth Murphy, Sara Riemersma, Amanda Halash, Alicia Kasen, and Brad Hill, who always go above and beyond to bring rich, beautiful, Christ-centered writing to this world.

This book wouldn't exist without the unwavering support of my beloved, Leif Oines, who anchored me through the highs and lows of its creation. What we saw and experienced was beyond belief— "brutiful" and all—and there's no one I'd rather do this life with than you. I love you.

To all who contributed, prayed, and believed in this project, your impact resonates deeply. *The God You Need to Know* is not just a book; it's a testament to the Spirit working through community and the faith that sustains us all. Thank you.

BREATH PRAYERS

 Breath Prayer

BREATHE IN:

Spirit of the Living God

BREATHE OUT:

I want all of you.

 Breath Prayer

BREATHE IN:

Spirit of the Living God

BREATHE OUT:

Move mightily in my mayhem.

Breath Prayer

BREATHE IN:

Spirit of the Living God

BREATHE OUT:

Help me hear from you, both day and night.

 Breath Prayer

BREATHE IN:

Spirit of the Living God

BREATHE OUT:

Use what I make to make a difference.

 Breath Prayer

BREATHE IN:

Spirit of the Living God

BREATHE OUT:

Wear me like a garment.

Breath Prayer

BREATHE IN:

Spirit of the Living God

BREATHE OUT:

Be ever on my lips.

Breath Prayer

BREATHE IN:

Spirit of the Living God

BREATHE OUT:

Sustain me while I wait.

Breath Prayer

BREATHE IN:

Spirit of the Living God

BREATHE OUT:

All I have is yours.

Breath Prayer

BREATHE IN:

Spirit of the Living God

BREATHE OUT:

Wherever you lead, I'll go.

 Breath Prayer

BREATHE IN:

Spirit of the Living God

BREATHE OUT:

Use me to bring healing to this divided world.

REFLECTION QUESTIONS FOR DISCERNMENT

WHEN YOU SENSE A PROMPTING of the Spirit, it's an invitation to a conversation with God—an opportunity to pray and reflect. Here are some questions to consider as you sort through the discernment process:

01	IS THE PROMPTING CONSISTENT WITH SCRIPTURE?	YES ❏	NO ❏
02	IS THE PROMPTING CONSISTENT WITH THE CHARACTER OF GOD?	YES ❏	NO ❏
03	DOES THE PROMPTING OF THE SPIRIT ALIGN WITH THE WORK GOD HAS ALREADY BEEN DOING IN YOUR LIFE?	YES ❏	NO ❏

Reflection Questions for Discernment

---

04   IS THE PROMPTING A RESPONSE, OR EVEN A PARTIAL RESPONSE, TO THE PRAYERS YOU'VE BEEN PRAYING?

YES ❏   NO ❏

---

05   WILL YOUR OBEDIENCE INCREASE YOUR DEPENDENCE ON GOD?

YES ❏   NO ❏

---

06   DO THE PROMPTING AND YOUR RESPONSE CAUSE YOU TO LOVE GOD OR OTHERS (AND PREFERABLY BOTH) MORE?

YES ❏   NO ❏

---

07   IS WHAT YOU BELIEVE YOU'VE HEARD FROM THE SPIRIT BLANKETED IN LOVE?

YES ❏   NO ❏

---

08   IF APPROPRIATE, DOES YOUR RESPONSE ALIGN WITH THE WISE COUNSEL IN YOUR LIFE?

YES ❏   NO ❏

---

09   DOES WHAT YOU HEARD LEAVE YOU WITH A SENSE OF PEACE?

YES ❏   NO ❏

FIRST CORINTHIANS 13 IN THE DISCERNMENT PROCESS

FIRST CORINTHIANS 13 includes a beautiful list of characteristics describing what it looks like when love is lived out. We can discern the Spirit's prompting and our response by using this powerful passage. The list of questions below is based on 1 Corinthians 13 and designed to help us evaluate whether our response will ultimately lead us to exhibiting God's lavish love.

As you read each question, simply tick "Yes" if you agree or "No" if you disagree.

---

01   DOES EVERYTHING I'M SENSING TO SAY OR DO DEMONSTRATE LOVE?

YES ❏   NO ❏

---

02   WILL WHAT I'M ABOUT TO SAY OR DO EMBODY PATIENCE AND KINDNESS?

YES ❏   NO ❏

First Corinthians 13 in the Discernment Process

		YES	NO
03	WILL SAYING OR DOING THIS LEAD ME TO PRIORITIZE OTHERS' NEEDS OVER MY OWN?	☐	☐
04	WILL MY RESPONSE DISCOURAGE ME FROM FOSTERING INTERNAL FEELINGS OF JEALOUSY, ARROGANCE, OR A DESIRE TO SHOW OFF?	☐	☐
05	WILL MY CHOSEN WORDS OR ACTIONS RESULT IN OTHERS FEELING RESPECTED, APPRECIATED, AND HONORED?	☐	☐
06	WILL MY CHOICE TO SAY OR DO THIS GUIDE ME TOWARD A MORE SELFLESS AND OTHERS-ORIENTED LIFE?	☐	☐
07	DOES WHAT I'M SENSING TO SAY OR DO PROMOTE CALM AND LEAD ME AWAY FROM ANGER?	☐	☐
08	DOES MY RESPONSE HELP ME RESIST THE URGE TO KEEP SCORE OF OTHERS' WEAKNESSES?	☐	☐
09	WILL MY WORDS OR ACTIONS CAUSE ME TO TRUST GOD MORE AND LOOK FOR THE BEST IN OTHERS?	☐	☐
10	WILL SAYING OR DOING THIS ENHANCE MY ABILITY TO LOVE IN A WAY THAT PROTECTS, TRUSTS, AND NEVER GIVES UP?	☐	☐

ABOUT
THE COVER

MORE THAN ANYTHING, I WANTED this book's cover to reflect my personal discovery as I studied the Holy Spirit—namely, the Spirit appears frequently throughout the Old Testament but for much of my life, I didn't recognize the Spirit's presence.

It reminded me of the children's magazine *Highlights*, which included a page of "Hidden Pictures" in each issue. Readers were invited to find small hidden images within a larger drawing.

As a kid, I'd find a pair of eyeglasses amid leaves on a tree or a drumstick as one of the legs of a table. In the same way, once we begin to look for the Holy Spirit in the Old Testament, we find the Spirit's presence and handiwork throughout.

The incredible design team at Zondervan, led by Curt Diepenhorst, took a huge risk by allowing me to try to create this concept. I had no idea how. But I thought if anyone on the planet could possibly pull off the creation of this cover, it's my sweet florist friend Susie, of Willow and Sage Floral Design.

I shared my vision for the cover, along with my doubts, and she said, "Margaret, we've got to *go* for it!" She hunted for the most colorful flowers we could possibly find and gathered with a photographer in a tiny home office to create an arrangement that contained hidden elements from the book—just like *Highlights*'s "Hidden Pictures."

If you look extra close at the cover, you'll see them:

- Water droplets on leaves—a reminder of the Spirit who hovers over the deep.

- Feathers tucked throughout—a reminder of the Spirit's presence and who speaks even when our heads hit the pillow.

- Flowers—reminders that the Spirit uses what we make to make a difference.

- Fabric toward the base—a reminder that the Spirit wears us like a garment.

- The sword's handle—a reminder that the Spirit rests on our lips and sometimes it's time to put down our swords.

- The piece of driftwood—a reminder that the Spirit works in the waiting, as my parents discovered while building a cottage on a remote island.

About the Cover

- A slice of pomegranate—a reminder that the Spirit wastes nothing, and even what appears insignificant can be redeemed.

- The vibrant, colorful, diverse arrangement—a reminder that there's no telling what might happen when we answer the Spirit's prompting to "go."

- A ruby earring—a reminder that the Spirit heals divides, even when it involves a famous jewel thief.

Now that you know the backstory of the cover, I'd love for you to take The God You Need to Know Challenge on page 199.

THE GOD YOU NEED TO KNOW CHALLENGE

IF YOU'VE READ THE About the Cover section, then you know that there's so much more tucked into the cover of this book than first meets the eye. You can do The God You Need to Know Challenge on your own, or better yet, gather with a friend or two who have read this book, too!

Here's the idea: What if you gathered with a friend or two and put in your floral or vegetation arrangement items that reflect the ways the Holy Spirit has worked in each of your lives?

What elements represent the way the Holy Spirit has hovered over you, led you, spoken to you, worked in your waiting, and healed you?

I'd love to see what you create! May we show the world

the power and presence of the Holy Spirit in our lives? Would you put together an image of the Spirit's work in your life, snap a picture, post online? Add the tag #TheGodYouNeedtoKnowBook and tag me on Instagram at @mafeinberg or Facebook at @margaretfeinberg or simply send an email to hello@margaretfeinberg.com.

I can't wait to hear from you!

MEET MARGARET

MARGARET FEINBERG IS A RADIANT soul whose laughter and boundless enthusiasm have earned her a reputation as someone who doesn't just teach about joy—she embodies it.

Growing up with an artist's heart, a storyteller's mind, and a journalist's curiosity, Margaret has spent most of her life inspiring others to live with wide-eyed faith, unbridled joy, and a deep sense of wonder when it comes to God and Scripture. Because, as she so often reminds us, God's presence is all around—if we'll just pause long enough to delight in the One who delights in us.

Host of the podcast *The Joycast*, Margaret is a Bible teacher and speaker at churches and leading conferences. Her books and Bible studies, including *Scouting the Divine*, *Fight Back With Joy*, *Taste and See*, and *Revelation: Extravagant Hope*, have sold well over a million copies and received critical acclaim and extensive media coverage from *USA Today*, *Los Angeles Times*, *The Washington Post*, and more. She was even named one of fifty women most shaping culture and the church today by *Christianity Today*.

Meet Margaret

When she's not writing or speaking at gatherings across the globe, you'll likely find Margaret making creative messes throughout the house, swimming like a dolphin at her local pool, or laughing around the table with friends, her husband Leif, and their forever puppy, Zoom.

Margaret loves connecting with readers online and through speaking at live events. Whether you have a heartfelt or whimsy message to send or you're planning an event, she'd love to connect!

Feel free to drop her a note at hello@margaretfeinberg.com.

NOTES

Chapter 1: Searching for the Spirit

8 *with* Christ *in* God: Colossians 3:3.

9 "*men* and *women* alike": Joel 2:28–29 NLT, italics added.

14 wind blows: John 3:8.

14 from Jesus's exhale: John 20:22.

15 fan of brief prayers: Matthew 6:7–8.

Chapter 2: The Spirit Who Hovers

19 heavens and the earth: Genesis 1:1.

19 over the waters: Genesis 1:2, italics added.

26 feel like devastation: Trevor Burke and Keith Warrington, eds., *A Biblical Theology of the Holy Spirit* (Eugene: Cascade Press, 2014), 3. Here, Walter Kaiser notes that *tohu* also has the connotation of desert waste (Deuteronomy 32:10; Job 6:18; 12:24), a lonely, desperate devastation. Isaiah uses *tohu* in the context of total devastation (Isaiah 24:10; 34:11).

27 *hovering* over the waters: Genesis 1:2, italics added.

27 "flutter": Rabbi Rachel Timoner, *Breath of Life: God as Spirit in Judaism* (Brewster: Paraclete Press, 2011), 5.

27 "*hovers* over its young": Deuteronomy 32:11, italics added. This reference is the only other use of *merahephet* in the Old Testament.

28 throughout our neighborhoods: At first, I foolishly

misunderstood eagles. I'd noticed salmon left on the sides, and sometimes in the middle, of the roads. Not only was the scent of decomposing fish carcasses overpowering, but the fish left large oily spots on the streets, which made sudden stops dangerous. I couldn't figure out why people in town were so irresponsible as to throw salmon wherever they wanted, but I figured that's just how they did it in Alaska. One day I was driving with Leif and complained about all the people throwing their leftover salmon everywhere. He laughed heartily and explained that it wasn't the people, it was the eagles. Turns out that when eagles are fishing, their eyes are sometimes bigger than their talons (much like me with a buffet). They'll grab a jumbo salmon from the water, but the farther they travel, the fish might slip, leaving salmon splats in the streets around town.

28 keep them snuggly warm: Alaska Raptor Center, "Bald Eagle 'Brood Patch,'" YouTube video, May 12, 2021, https://www .youtube.com/watch?v=DvgAw9IHX3w; "Bald Eagle Nestling Facts," Journey North, accessed December 17, 2024, https://journeynorth.org/tm/eagle/annual/facts_nestlings.html. The imagery in Deuteronomy 32:11 just keeps getting richer as God spreads his wings, rescues any falling children, and soars with them resting on his wings.

28 "will rescue it": Isaiah 31:5.

28 under her wings: Luke 13:34.

29 "will *overshadow* you": Luke 1:35, italics added.

29 overshadows the temple: Exodus 40:35, Septuagint.

29 "Listen to Him!": Burke and Warrington, *A Biblical Theology of the Holy Spirit*, 5. Scripture reference is Mark 9:7.

Chapter 3: The Spirit While We Sleep

36 "give it to you": 1 Kings 3:5–15.

36 few of his own: Daniel 2; 4; 7:1–14.

36 chapter of Acts: Joel 2:28–32; Acts 2:17–18.

36 where to return home: Matthew 1:20–23; 2:13–14, 19–20, 22–23.

36 once and for all: Matthew 27:19–24.

Notes

37 how to respond: In addition to dreams, the Bible contains many accounts of visions and waking trances, including Paul's nighttime vision of the man from Macedonia, Cornelius and Peter in Acts 10, and John's visit to the heavenly realms throughout Revelation.

42 repelled by its odiousness: Genesis 37; 39–50.

43 even they are incredulous: My friend Tracee shared with me Rembrandt's *Joseph Telling His Dreams*. It's worth viewing online. Notice in the bottom left corner rests a small dog licking himself. It seems to capture what the brothers are thinking in such a funny way.

45 "Spirit of God abides": Genesis 41:38 BSB.

46 future descendants: Genesis 15:12–16.

46 lay a finger on her: Genesis 20:3–7.

46 ladder stretching to heaven: Genesis 28:12–13.

47 researchers have found: Joshua Rapp Learn, "What Foods Can Give You Nightmares?," *Discover Magazine*, December 8, 2022, https://www.discovermagazine.com/mind/what-foods-can -give-you-nightmares.

47 also heals us: Matthew Walker, "Why Your Brain Needs to Dream," *Greater Good Magazine*, October 24, 2017, https://greatergood.berkeley.edu/article/item /why_your_brain_needs_to_dream.

47 already promised us: James 1:5.

53 "I did not know it": Genesis 28:16 ESV.

Chapter 4: The Artisan Spirit

59 home-team victory: Exodus 17:8–16.

60 See, I have chosen: Exodus 31:2–5, italics added.

62 complementary skills: Exodus 38:23.

62 "ability to teach others": Exodus 35:34.

64 "to make": Exodus 31:4, 6.

64 diversity of spiritual gifts: 1 Corinthians 12:4–6.

65 Willow and Sage Floral Design: willowandsagefloral.com. Susie also has a beautiful book, *The Failure of God: Honesty About Faith*, that will encourage and breathe life into your soul.

67 "Pieces": Steffany Gretzinger, vocalist, "Pieces," by Amanda Lindsey Cook and Steffany Dawn Gretzinger, track 6 on Bethel Music, *Have It All*, Bethel Music, 2016.

69 "in remembrance of me": Luke 22:19.

Chapter 5: The Spirit Who Wears Us Well

73 "Forty more days": Jonah 3:4.

73 long-overdue deep cleaning: 2 Chronicles 29:15–16. Any work that brings people to God is prompted by the Spirit.

74 over one hundred years: Five years after Count Zinzendorf opened his land to refugees, more than three hundred people had moved onto his property. Despite their differences, they prayed for a spiritual outpouring seven days a week, twenty-four hours a day, for a century. They became a wellspring sending people to share the news of Jesus around the world.

75 three hundred thousand: Greg Laurie, "America's Great Awakenings," Harvest, September 5, 2018, https://harvest.org /resources/devotion/americas-great-awakenings-2/.

75 Second Great Awakening: Some historians attribute the rise of abolitionists fighting against slavery in the United States to this awakening.

81 cumbersome codes: Matthew 23:1–4.

82 brutal Midianites: Numbers 31:7–18 and Judges 6:1–6. The Midianite population, once diminished under Joshua, has surged again.

82 This is what the Lord: Judges 6:8–10, italics added. It's worth noting that God uses the same opening words here that he does for the Ten Commandments.

84 "mighty warrior": Judges 6:12.

84 "Go in the strength": Judges 6:14.

85 "The Lord Is Peace": Judges 6:24.

85 *Then the Spirit*: Judges 6:34–35, italics added.

86 "clothed himself": Christopher J. H. Wright in his wonderful book, *Knowing the Holy Spirit Through the Old Testament* (Downers

Grove: InterVarsity Press, 2006), writes, "God's Spirit put Gideon on like a coat!" (40).

86 like a garment: Not only does the Spirit wear us, but the Spirit also clothes us. Colossians 3:12 instructs us, "Therefore, as God's chosen people, holy and dearly loved, clothe yourselves with compassion, kindness, humility, gentleness and patience." In other words, we are to be clothed with the fruit of the Spirit. And how is this possible? Because we are clothed in Christ (Galatians 3:27)!

86 "If *you* will save": Judges 6:36, italics added.

87 battle protocols: Deuteronomy 20:8.

87 "A sword for the LORD": Judges 7:20.

88 One who wears it: Acts 17:28.

88 who lives in us: John 14:17; Romans 8:11; 1 Corinthians 6:19; 1 John 4:4, 13, 15.

93 "that they all may be one": John 17:21 KJV.

Chapter 6: The Spirit Who Speaks Through Us

95 year of chemotherapy: My yearlong journey of treatment and discovering God's graces along the way is told in the book and Bible study *Fight Back with Joy: Celebrate More. Regret Less. Stare Down Your Greatest Fear* (Worthy, 2015).

97 "God whispers to us": C. S. Lewis, *The Problem of Pain* (New York: HarperCollins, 2001), 90–91.

98 "For the battle": 2 Chronicles 20:15.

98 "it is very good": Genesis 1:3, 6, 14, 18, 21, 31.

99 "a man after God's own heart": 1 Samuel 13:14; Acts 13:22.

99 "the Spirit of the LORD": 1 Samuel 16:13 ESV.

99 rushed upon Saul too: 1 Samuel 10:10.

100 the last words of David: 2 Samuel 23:1 describes David's words as his last, meaning his last significant public speech, though technically, David does speak again in 1 Kings 2:1–9.

100 The Spirit of the LORD: 2 Samuel 23:2.

100 "speaking by the Spirit": Matthew 22:43. Jesus quotes David: "The LORD says to my lord: 'Sit at my right hand until I make your enemies a footstool for your feet'" (Psalm 110:1). This psalm

is crucial in the formation of New Testament Christology and the understanding of Jesus as God. Also, this is the most widely used or quoted psalm in the New Testament across all genres. David's words provided a pillar on which much of New Testament Christology rests.

100 Amasai: 1 Chronicles 12:18.

100 seventy elders: Numbers 11:25–26.

100 Balaam: Numbers 24:2–3.

100 spark reform and repentance: 2 Chronicles 15:1–15.

100 "Do not be afraid": 2 Chronicles 20:15.

101 Deborah, Zechariah, Huldah, Isaiah, Ezekiel, and Micah: Judges 4:4; 2 Chronicles 24:20; 2 Chronicles 34:22–33; Isaiah 48:15–17; Ezekiel 11:14–17; Micah 3:8.

101 "spoke from God": 2 Peter 1:21.

101 filled with the Spirit: Luke 1:41–42.

101 form of song: Luke 1:46–55.

101 Elizabeth's husband, Zechariah: Luke 1:67–70. It's interesting to think about the Lord's taking his speech from him for nine months and giving him the gift of thinking about his words.

101 turn back to God: Luke 1:16–17.

101 life-giving speech: Proverbs 18:21.

101 fountain of life: Proverbs 10:11.

101 wise brings healing: Proverbs 12:18

101 righteous nourish many: Proverbs 10:21.

102 gift of the Holy Spirit: Acts 2:38.

102 "God-breathed": 2 Timothy 3:16 NIV and MSG.

104 If I speak: 1 Corinthians 13:1–3, italics added.

Chapter 7: The Spirit Who Works in the Waiting

112 When Moses is tapped: Exodus 4:10.

112 When Jeremiah discovers: Jeremiah 1:6.

112 when Isaiah receives: Isaiah 6:11.

112 serve in the temple: Numbers 4:1–4; Ezekiel 1:3.

113 Spirit lifts him: Ezekiel 2:2.

113 fall on deaf ears: Ezekiel 3:7–9.

113 deep distress: Ezekiel 3:14–15.

114 "Can these bones live?": Ezekiel 37:3.

114 he invites Ezekiel: Ezekiel 37:4–6.

114 as I was prophesying: Ezekiel 37:7–8, "*ruach*" substituted for "breath" in the NIV text.

115 "There was no *ruach*": Ezekiel 37:8.

115 "Prophesy to the *ruach*": Ezekiel 37:9–10, "*ruach*" substituted for "breath," "winds," and "breathe" in the NIV text; *ruchot* is plural of *ruach*.

116 *The Spirit of God*: Romans 8:11 NLT, italics added.

Chapter 8: The Spirit Who Wastes Nothing

128 King Zedekiah of Judah: 2 Kings 24:18–25:21.

130 gained through injustice: Daniel 4:27.

130 actually *gains* weight: Daniel 1:15.

130 God *gave* these four: Daniel 1:17 HCSB, italics added.

130 "suitable for instruction": Daniel 1:4 HCSB, italics added.

131 In every matter: Daniel 1:20, italics added.

132 The *ruach* of the holy gods is in him: Daniel 4:8.

132 I know that the *ruach*: Daniel 4:9.

132 The *ruach* of the holy gods is in you: Daniel 4:18.

132 he describes Babylon: Daniel 4:30, italics added.

132 He's driven away: Daniel 4:28–37 tells the story of the king's transformation.

135 "The steps of a man": Psalm 37:23 NASB.

135 experience, backgrounds, and interests: The spectacular but surprising result of this mixing is one of the reasons the writer of Hebrews exhorts us to be together (Hebrews 10:24–25).

Chapter 9: The Spirit Who Says "Go"

140 "how should I pray?": For many years I've loved a detail from the Lord's Prayer as related in the Gospel of Luke. One day after Jesus had been praying in a particular place, a disciple whose name we don't know approaches Jesus and says, "Lord, teach us to pray" (Luke 11:1). Jesus answers with what's fondly known as the Lord's

Prayer. But that request—"Lord, teach us to pray"—could be a prayer we desire to pray for a person, situation, or even ourselves. The Spirit sits ready to align our words, our desires, our longings with God's. Oh, and this couple and I developed a friendship that lasted many years.

145 *go*: I often turn to BibleGateway.com for research, and when I typed in "go," the biblical search engine revealed zero results. I wrote the website's team and asked if this might be an oversight. They explained that two-letter words hadn't been integrated into their system—but they'd fix it as fast as they could. I'm grateful, because without the word *go* we'd miss out on so much of what the Spirit wants to do in us and through us. I turned to a different search engine and was soon overwhelmed by the frequency of the command to "go" throughout the Bible. What's even more amazing is how often the Lord uses other terms to nudge and prompt us to action.

146 Noah: Genesis 7:1.

146 Abram: Genesis 12:1.

146 Aaron: Exodus 4:27.

146 Balaam: Numbers 22:35; 23:16.

146 Moses: Exodus 6:11; 8:1; 9:1; 10:1. Moses received so many commands to "go," it's a little mind-boggling: Exodus 4:19; 17:5; 19:10; 19:21; 32:7.

146 Deborah: Judges 4:6.

146 Gideon: Judges 6:14.

146 David: 1 Chronicles 14:10.

146 Nathan: 1 Chronicles 17:3–4.

146 Gad: 1 Chronicles 21:9–10.

146 Elijah: 1 Kings 18:1; 19:11, 15.

146 Isaiah: Isaiah 6:8–9; 7:3; 22:15; 38:5.

146 Jeremiah: Jeremiah 2:2; 3:12; 13:1; 17:19; 19:1; 22:1; 28:13; 34:2; 35:2; 35:13; 39:16.

146 Ezekiel: Ezekiel 3:24; 8:9.

146 Hosea: Hosea 1:2; 3:1.

146 Amos: Amos 7:15.

146 Holy Spirit whispers: Based on Luke 2:26.

146 The LORD will lay bare: Isaiah 52:10. Simeon is such a beautiful example of one who grounded himself in study and the Spirit. As Simeon's song later reveals, he is saturated with the promises of Isaiah 40–55. In *Fresh Air: The Holy Spirit for an Inspired Life* (Paraclete Press, 2012), Jack Levison explores Simeon's song through Isaiah's words and it's stunning. I highly recommend the entire book.

147 "moved by the Spirit": Luke 2:27.

147 hours for study: I'm having some fun here with the story.

147 Mary and Joseph: Mary and Joseph also know what it's like to be nudged to go somewhere. An angel of the Lord appears to Joseph in a dream and instructs him to take his wife, Mary, and the newborn and escape to Egypt (Matthew 2:13). After the bloodthirsty King Herod dies, an angel of the Lord appears to Joseph again and tells him to go back to Israel (Matthew 2:19–20).

148 sacrifice for her purification: Leviticus 12.

148 baby boy's dedication: Exodus 13:2.

149 Sovereign Lord: Luke 2:29–30.

149 This child is destined: Luke 2:34–35.

150 1 Corinthians 13: I developed a helpful list called First Corinthians 13 in the Discernment Process on pages 193–194.

158 in step with the Spirit: Galatians 5:25.

158 Therefore *go*: Matthew 28:19–20, italics added.

Chapter 10: The Spirit Who Heals Divides

163 American Museum of Natural History: Meryl Gordon, "The 50th Anniversary of New York's Most Sensational Jewel Heist," *Vanity Fair*, October 29, 2014, https://www.vanityfair.com/style /scandal/2014/10/museum-of-natural-history-jewel-heist; and https://www.youtube.com/watch?v=DZnHMpVLwFk.

163 two life sentences: "Florida Won't Restore Rights of Famed Jewel Thief," *Tampa Bay Times*, December 13, 2012, https://www.tampabay.com/news/publicsafety/crime /florida-wont-restore-rights-of-famed-jewel-thief/1266090/.

166 heart-wrenching cry: Matthew 27:46 and Mark 15:34, quoting our friend David, on whose lips the Spirit rested, in Psalm 22:1.

167 And I will ask: John 14:16, italics added.

168 empowered the seventy: Luke 10:1–17.

168 helped raise Jesus: Romans 8:11.

169 underscores their unity: Acts 2:1, italics added.

169 cleansed Isaiah's lips: Isaiah 6:6–7.

169 never spoken before: Acts 2:6–12.

169 traces the work: Acts 2:13–41.

169 Spirit-infused speech: Acts 7–8:1.

170 carries a singular message: Acts 8:4–8.

170 (formerly) lost puppy: Now, after years in the dark arts, Simon still has a thing or two to learn the hard way, basics like the Holy Spirit can't be purchased or reduced to a multilevel-marketing, money-making scheme. When confronted with his mistaken beliefs, Simon asks for prayer, recognizing he has a long way to go.

170 crushed or cut off: While Jesus once spoke of eunuchs who had been that way since birth, more commonly, eunuchs in antiquity were prisoners of war or slaves whose man bits had been crushed or cut off. The Torah regulated that those who had been mutilated were forbidden to participate in temple rituals (Deuteronomy 23:1; Matthew 19:11–12).

171 participation in communal life: John W. Martens, "Is the Ethiopian Eunuch the First Gentile Convert in Acts?," *America Magazine*, September 23, 2015, https://www.americamagazine.org/content/good-word/acts-apostles-online-commentary-25.

171 eunuch's baptism: Now, in the Gospels and Acts, the standard order of events is that a person is called to turn to God and then instructed to get baptized. Here the script is flipped. The eunuch readily receives the good news of Jesus, and then he's the one who initiates the baptism.

171 Ananias: Acts 9:10–17.

171 Barnabas: Acts 9:26–28.

171 Cornelius: Acts 10. Cornelius served as a high-ranking commander in the Roman military—the same army that used

their power and status to impoverish swaths of the Jewish
population.

172 every new friendship: Acts 2:4; 9:10, 12; 10:3, 17, 19; 11:5, 16:9;
18:9. Examples include Ananias, Cornelius, Peter, and Paul.

175 "added to their number": Acts 2:47.

177 never thought possible: Barbara Brown Taylor, *Home by Another
Way* (Rowman & Littlefield, 1997), 143.

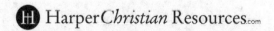

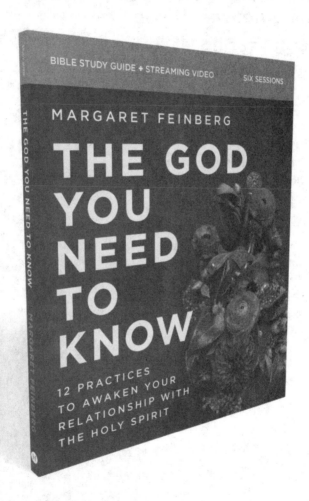

One of Margaret's greatest joys is speaking to live audiences. If you have a gathering of 250 or more, consider her for your next event.

Simply email:
booking@margaretfeinberg.com
for more details.